Managerial Communication
for the Arabian Gulf

Managerial Communication for the Arabian Gulf

Valerie Priscilla Goby, Catherine Nickerson, and Chrysi Rapanta

BEP BUSINESS EXPERT PRESS

Managerial Communication for the Arabian Gulf

Copyright © Business Expert Press, LLC, 2016.

First published in 2016 by
Business Expert Press, LLC
222 East 46th Street, New York, NY 10017
www.businessexpertpress.com

ISBN-13: 978-1-63157-246-3 (paperback)
ISBN-13: 978-1-63157-247-0 (e-book)

Business Expert Press Corporate Communication Collection

Collection ISSN: 2156-8162 (print)
Collection ISSN: 2156-8170 (electronic)

Cover and interior design by Exeter Premedia Services Private Ltd., Chennai, India

First edition: 2016

10 9 8 7 6 5 4 3 2 1

Printed in the United States of America.

Abstract

This book presents a comprehensive account of management communication in the Arabian Gulf that will appeal to two different types of reader. First, managers on assignment, most especially those with little or no experience of the region, will find that it addresses many of the questions that are likely to arise as they attempt to manage diverse workforces within the region. Second, students of management, managerial communication, culture, and cross-cultural communication will benefit from the scholarly introduction it provides to these topics both in general and within the specific Gulf context. To bridge the interests of these two different groups, this volume provides an extensive set of concrete solutions and advice as well as an accessible discussion based on current academic research. Both types of readers will navigate these two strands easily and with interest. The book offers an overview of the diverse workforces of the Gulf, an introduction to culture in the Gulf, communication among different cultural groups within the workforce, and how best to achieve effective intercultural communication. It summarizes the different approaches to management that exist in the region and also looks at typical negotiation styles. The final chapter consists of case studies designed to provide a practical insight into a range of topics and problems relating to managerial communication in real-world Gulf situations.

Keywords

Arabian Gulf, cross-cultural communication, culture in the Arabian Gulf, leadership communication in the Arabian Gulf, management styles, managerial communication, negotiation strategies, women in the Arabian Gulf, workforce localization

Contents

Introduction

Our focus in this book is communication within the workplaces of the countries that form the Cooperation Council for the Arab States of the Gulf, with particular reference to managers. Originally, and still popularly, termed the GCC (Gulf Cooperation Council), its members include all the Arab states of the Persian Gulf with the exception of Iraq. The GCC was established in Abu Dhabi in 1981, and it consists of Bahrain, Kuwait, Oman, Saudi Arabia, the United Arab Emirates, and Qatar. It was set up to foster political, economic, military, scientific, cultural, legislative, and monetary links between its members. The member countries rank among those with the highest gross domestic products (GDPs) in the world and represent some of the world's fastest growing economies, all of which have benefitted from the exploitation of rich oil resources. In cultural terms, the region displays considerable shared identity with all the states being Arabic speaking and Muslim.

As of 2014, 28 of the 30 largest companies in the Arab world in terms of market capitalization were based in GCC countries.[1] Individual Gulf business people hold the largest overseas investments of all Arabs, and they are highly active investors throughout the Middle East region.[2] With a focus on diversifying business concerns beyond the oil industry and the creation of jobs in numerous commercial sectors within a successful knowledge economy, an enormous range of public and private sector companies have been established, many of which have foreign management. Not only is business expanding; so too is the region's population, which now registers the highest rate of growth in the world.[3] This increased from 10 million in 1975 to over 50 million in 2010, and about 30 to 70 percent of the population of each member state is made up of expatriates[4] who migrated to the GCC to work on the development of infrastructure following the oil boom.[5] While there is widespread concern over this demographic imbalance,[6] the GCC countries continue to have the highest rates of migrant workers in the world and the highest rates of remittances to foreign workers' home countries.[7] The massive number of workers hailing from more than 200 different countries, the drive toward economic diversification, and the effort to incorporate more local workers into the private sectors mean that managers are challenged by a workplace that is likely to be far more complex than those they have previously encountered. So while managers across the globe typically have to wear many hats, in the Gulf they may find that they need to wear many more than they are used to.

The book begins with a chapter detailing the unique makeup of the modern-day labor force in the Gulf. It explains the historical context, most notably the discovery of oil and the subsequent importing of overseas labor. It goes on to outline the various localization policies that exist across the region and the effect of these on the workforce. These government-backed initiatives aim to redress the imbalance between the small number of Gulf citizens who are part of the workforce and the enormous numbers of expatriate employees, particularly in the private sector. The initiatives also actively encourage local women into the workforce and recognize their contribution to future social and economic development. An awareness of the composition of the workforce is crucial to understanding workplace communication.

Chapter 2 identifies the cultural trends that are prevalent in the Gulf region and looks at both local cultures and the cultures of those nations that make up the bulk of the expatriate labor force. In our discussion, we refer to the well-known work by the social psychologist Geert Hofstede[8] and show how national culture determines how people view different aspects of both social and corporate life, such as their attitudes to hierarchy, groups, rules, time, and ambition.

Having outlined the composition of the workforce and the cultural variables that are likely to influence how individual workers behave, Chapter 3 discusses in detail how these variables influence work-based communication. Much of this chapter is focused on the work of the anthropologist Edward Hall[9] and his construct of high and low context cultures. In brief, his model broadly describes the culture and communication that are prevalent in the Eastern world, defined as high context, and the culture and communication that are customary in the Western world, termed low context. Our discussion on important differences between the high context cultures of the Gulf workforce and the low context cultures of many Western countries includes relationship building, the concepts of honor and face, nonverbal communication, directness versus indirectness, ambiguity, and speaking versus writing.

Chapter 4 presents an examination of intercultural communication with a focus on how managers can communicate successfully with multicultural workforces to achieve work goals. In this chapter, we consider the role played by English as a business lingua franca in the region and its relationship with Arabic. We describe how speakers can promote successful communication by accommodating each other if they are both speaking a language that is not their first language. We also discuss how effective communicators manage work-based discussions by creating rapport with the people with whom they are interacting.

In Chapter 5, we look at the communication styles that Gulf people tend to prefer. These styles may appear to Westerners as circular and repetitive rather than linear, which is the pattern usually favored in Western contexts. We discuss how negotiations in the Gulf region are typically characterized by compromise and a willingness to hold lengthy discussions in order to preserve existing business relationships, rather than risking confrontation by quickly moving toward a conclusion.

Chapter 6 presents an overview of management styles in the Gulf and addresses the need to manage diversity within the workforce. Here we also discuss the changing nature of leadership and leadership communication styles and the emergence of women leaders in the region. Chapter 7 offers a collection of cases that focus on particular aspects of workforce communication and management in the Gulf. These include the integration of locals within the expatriate-dominated private sectors of the region, business etiquette, the use of business English, diversity climate, negotiation styles, and management styles and practices.

CHAPTER 1

The Gulf Workforce

The Gulf countries have the highest proportion of migrant workers in the world, and the immigrants send a large amount of remittances back home.[1]

The huge changes that have taken place in the Gulf Cooperation Council (GCC) in the past few decades have made the business world there unique. Even managers with wide experience in multinational corporations (MNCs) may be unfamiliar with the nature of the GCC workforces and business practices. In this chapter, we examine features of the Gulf workforce that have a significant impact on workplace communication. Our review will provide a background to some of the complexities of the region's work environment.

Historic Reliance on Imported Labor

The dramatic economic changes in the Arabian Gulf following the oil boom are well known. Evolving from a region of desert tribes and small port towns with limited formal schooling opportunities for its citizens, the Gulf has undergone exponential socioeconomic change in recent decades. As the economy surged, ample funding was directed to building much-needed infrastructures. However, the region's small and poorly educated population could not supply the labor needed to satisfy the expanding workforce. The response was to import labor from all over the globe, but most especially from the nearby Indian subcontinent. Salaries were made as tempting as needed, resulting in considerable variation determined by potential home-country earnings. These foreign workers soon outnumbered the local populations, and currently the region has the highest rate of migrant workers in the world.[2] The result is a group of countries in which the local populations represent a minority within a workforce comprised of as many as 220 different nationalities.

Since the 1970s, numerous metropolises have sprung up in the region. Millions of young Gulf nationals have graduated from educational establishments into which vast sums of money are poured as governments endeavor to develop educated populations in keeping with their countries' economic and social advancement. Many MNCs have established operations in the region, lured by the abundance of cheap imported labor from Asia, the absence of corporate or personal taxation, the unrestricted movement of capital, and the high-quality infrastructures.

Local Workforces

Over the past 50 years, mandatory school attendance and funding for further studies both locally and overseas have resulted in the various countries in the region producing a large number of local high school and university graduates. However, the natural process by which these educated locals might have been expected to replace imported labor has not occurred. Government sector positions are frequently preferred by the local populations and regarded as a suitable way for them to contribute to their countries' development, and the private sector continues to be dominated by expatriate workers.

As the stream of local graduates increases and available public sector positions are filled, unemployment among locals has become an issue for some GCC governments. Growing populations and increasing youth unemployment in much of the Gulf have set the stage for social concerns that challenge governments in the region.[3] The dual needs to provide employment to locals and to allow them to take a central role in building up their countries' economies have been addressed by workforce localization policies directed largely at the private sectors.[4] These policies, set in place throughout the GCC, have seen varying degrees of success. However, foreign labor continues to dominate to a greater or lesser degree and the issue of demographic imbalance remains under close scrutiny.[5] The following sections provide a brief snapshot of localization by country.

Localization Policies

Bahrain: Bahrainization

The Kingdom of Bahrain, with a population of 1.2 million of which just over half are citizens,[6] implemented its localization policy in 1989. This required private sector companies to employ a certain quota of locals and also offer them higher salaries to help ensure that private sector positions would be as attractive to locals as public sector ones. In 2006, the Crown Prince developed further labor and economic reforms, the aim of which was to curtail the continuing preference of companies to employ cheaper foreign labor and to encourage the recruitment of local workers. To enhance the competitiveness of nationals in the labor market, a training authority called Tamkeen was established as part of Bahrain's Economic Vision.[7]

These reforms, however, were unpopular with business since they increased staffing costs and resulted in an increase in illegal workers within the Kingdom.[8] Nonetheless, before the political turmoil of 2011, Bahrain was heralded as one of the most successful of the Gulf countries in terms of integrating its locals into the private sector.[9] Following the political unrest of 2011 with its large-scale protests and strikes organized by the General Federation of Bahrain Trade Unions (GFBTU) and the subsequent declaration of a state of national security, labor reforms were modified to win support for government efforts from the influential business community. The government has also attempted to destabilize the power of the opposition-supporting GFBTU by permitting the establishment of more than one union per company. Given that these amendments to the localization policy reduce the cost of employing foreign workers and lower the minimum quotas of local hires, there is concern that they will further contribute to the mounting local youth unemployment and the country's labor problems.[10]

Kuwait: Kuwaitization

In the early 1980s, the Kuwaiti government introduced the Kuwaitization policy with the aim of equalizing the national and expatriate labor forces by the year 2000.[11] The 1985 Employment Bill required companies working under government contracts to employ 15 percent Kuwaitis in management and technical roles and 30 percent in other positions.[12] The relatively low educational level of many locals limits their competitiveness in the job market,[13] but the public sector continues to expand to accommodate Kuwaitis entering the job market. As a result, 75 percent of working Kuwaitis in 2013 were employed by the government.[14]

Despite over-employment in the public sector, now calculated at 50 percent, the government's capacity to continue to employ locals mitigates the need to foster private sector employment opportunities for them. Moreover, although 40 percent of Kuwaiti public sector employees do not have high school certificates, their salaries remain attractive. Kuwaitis make up only 2.3 percent of the private sector workforce, though almost half (0.9 percent) of this figure is comprised of females, which reflects gender equity not seen in other Gulf countries.[15]

Oman: Omanization

Oman also implemented an exhaustive effort to localize its workforce.[16] In 1996, the government launched its *Vision 2020* that consisted of a threefold policy: (1) diversification away from oil revenues, (2) privatization to reduce the prominence of the state, and (3) localization of its workforce. At that time, Omanis made up 44.7 percent of the total workforce with the highest rate (52.1 percent) in unskilled positions. However, with a young population and increasing numbers of graduates entering the job market, the skills level of locals improved, and by 2001, the banking sector, for example, had reached 90 percent Omanization.[17] As of 2014, Omanis made up 61 percent of the total workforce but are outnumbered six to one by expatriates in the private sector,[18] a trend which is likely to continue given that in the period from December 2012 to June 2014, the private sector hired twelve expatriates for every one Omani hired.[19]

Qatar: Qatarization

Qatar has the highest per capita gross domestic product (GDP) in the region and the smallest proportion of nationals within its total population of 2.1 million. Despite the 1997 decree mandating that Qataris constitute 20 percent of the private sector workforce, their participation now stands at only 0.3 percent.[20] It is the only country in the region in which expatriates outnumber local workers in the public sector, and localization efforts can still focus on this sector since it has the capacity to offer employment to all nationals wishing to work rather than having to involve the private sector in the employment of nationals. Qatari participation in the workforce is estimated to include 64.7 percent males and 34.6 percent females.[21] In 2014, the Ministry of Labor and Social Affairs established a committee to ensure a minimum of 20 percent localization within the private sector by 2019.[22]

Saudi Arabia: Saudization/Nitaqat

The 2007 census calculated the population of Saudi Arabia at 17.7 million, of whom 10.5 million were of working age. The government sector employs 760,000 Saudis, while the private sector employs 550,000 Saudis and 5.06 million foreigners.[23] An imperfectly developed education system has been identified as the reason for the poor preparedness of many nationals, and the localization policy has come under attack for forcing companies to employ unsuitably skilled locals who become a burden to the business community.[24] Cronyism in recruitment has also been cited as a major factor in the failure to match skills with positions.[25] A common view is that the country is too welfare-oriented to encourage the majority of nationals into the workforce,[26] and the government has been criticized for seeming to work against the private sector instead of with it in the localization initiative.[27]

United Arab Emirates: Emiratization

The United Arab Emirates (UAE) represents an appealing destination for MNCs, and in terms of ease of conducting business, it currently ranks 12th out of the 144 countries surveyed in the *Global Competitiveness Report*.[28] The country has made great strides in improving its educational systems, and its higher education system ranks 6th among the 144 countries surveyed for the report. However, its localization policies introduced in the 1990s have made little headway in increasing recruitment of locals to the private sector that is dominated by 98 percent expatriate workers. Unlike in other GCC countries, the public sector has reached saturation point; and this fact, coupled with the private sector's preference for foreign workers, has resulted in high unemployment among locals. The government unemployment figure is 15 percent,[29] but figures as high as 28 percent have been cited.[30]

Women in the Gulf Workforce

Interestingly, in much of the Gulf region, women frequently attain higher educational qualifications than do males and are hence seen as more desirable in the workforce. For example, of the total number of university graduates in Kuwait, Saudi Arabia, and Qatar, females represent 67 percent, 57 percent, and 56 percent, respectively. Nonetheless, largely due to cultural trends which prioritize the roles of mother and wife, the percentage of women in the GCC labor force is less than in other countries. In Qatar, 35 percent of women are in the workforce, with 28 percent in the UAE, and 12 percent in Saudi Arabia. These are low figures compared to the 79 percent of females who participate in the workforce in countries such as Norway and Switzerland.[31] Another significant issue for women in the Gulf workplace is the Islamic prohibition of interactions between unrelated men and women, which means that more conservative females will avoid applying for jobs in which they may be required to deal with male colleagues or customers.

The *Gender Gap Report*, prepared by the World Economic Forum since 2006, assesses the position of women across four subindexes, namely, economic participation and opportunity, educational attainment, health and survival, and political empowerment. Of the 142 countries surveyed for its 2014 report, Kuwait ranks 113th, the UAE, 115th, Qatar, 116th, Bahrain, 124th, Oman, 128th, and Saudi Arabia, 130th. In terms of the specific subindex of economic participation and opportunity, Qatar ranks 101st, Kuwait, 106th, Bahrain, 126th, Oman, 128th, the UAE, 123rd, and Saudi Arabia, 137th.[32]

However, the Gulf is not without some powerful female figures. The current UAE Minister for Foreign Trade, for example, Her Excellency

Sheikha Lubna Bint Khalid Al Qasimi, was recently ranked 42nd in *Forbes'* List of the World's 100 Most Powerful Women. She expresses a commonly held view on Gulf women's empowerment:

> The benefits of having women as agents for social change through taking a more visible role in society is not limited to paid employment [...]. These women, whether they are doctors or homemakers, are on the front lines of our community in transition.[33]

Kuwait has seen an increase in the presence of women-led nongovernmental organizations (NGOs) that focus on improving women's situation and facilitating their access to decision-making positions, not in the form of independent women's rights organizations, but as a part of the National Development Strategy. Qatar is also striving to empower women and increase their participation in leadership positions. Some efforts toward improving women's development opportunities are currently underway in Bahrain through the Supreme Council for Women. In various ways, GCC women's voices are now heard more than they have been in the past and their role in business is undoubtedly more prominent.

Common Concerns

While the GCC countries differ in terms of their workforce make-up and the opportunities and constraints that exist, some key factors relating to the local workforces apply across the GCC.

Entitlement?

Poor motivation on the part of Gulf locals has been the catch call of private sector organizations in their response to the criticism that they are doing little to recruit and retain local workers. Much attention is focused on the fact that locals from these countries with extremely high GDPs enjoy the luxury of a range of generous social welfare benefits. This "curse of entitlement," it is argued, has led to the development of a certain mindset in terms of how much local workers are prepared to do and for what salary.[34] The economic security they enjoy as citizens of high GDP countries makes it less attractive for them to enter the private sector or engage in entrepreneurship.[35] However, there is increasing evidence that a new breed of motivated graduates has sprung up in the Gulf, and they have shown themselves to be both qualified and willing to take the reins of their countries' economic development.[36]

False Implementation of Localization Requirements

The government directive to recruit a set percentage of locals in various sectors has led Gulf-based companies to find ways around this obligation. Many have developed fraudulent practices to allow them to continue operations as normal and avoid penalties for noncompliance while not, in fact, fulfilling the set quotas. The UAE, for example, has seen the advent of "ghost Emiratization" which refers to the practice of paying locals a monthly sum, usually about AED2,000 (US$545) to AED4,000 (US$1,090), to allow their names to appear on the company's list of employees even though they have never worked for the company. A variation of this practice is to offer local university students bursaries of a similar sum and classify them as employees even though no employment will ever be offered to them.[37]

In Oman, "fake Omanization" occurs whereby locals are hired simply to fulfill the given quota and thereby allow the hiring company to obtain a visa for a new expatriate worker.[38] In Saudi Arabia, private sector companies have been found to be fraudulently registering family members as employees.[39] Speculation in Kuwait is that as many as 20,000 Kuwaiti citizens are paid KD250 (US$825) per month to allow their names to be falsely included on companies' employee lists.

Two-Tier Workforce

Localization has established a particular workplace reality that managers have to cope with, namely, a two-tier workforce consisting of expatriates who are employed within the realm of a free labor market and locals who are often employed primarily to fulfill the quotas set by governments. The imbalance between expatriate workers from countries with low income potential and local workers whose expectations are naturally higher given the considerable economic health of their countries, makes for a starkly heterogeneous workforce.

Another significant issue is that the GCC countries rarely offer citizenship to foreign residents, regardless of the length of their residence in the country; so expatriate workers have little sense of long-term security. For the majority of Asians and those of other nationalities from countries with poor economic health and adverse work conditions, the opportunity of a job in the Gulf is highly prized and represents an enormous financial advantage over work in their home countries. This sense of advantage is strongly felt, as workers in many of their home countries suffer from deteriorating conditions and rights.[40] These facts make such members of the workforce highly compliant and keen to retain their positions at all costs.

On the other hand, locals are in a very different situation. As citizens, they have the right to residence regardless of their employment situation, they are often paid higher salaries as mandated by government regulation, they enjoy generous social welfare packages, and their dismissal is much more complicated than that of an expatriate worker. However, this does not mean that their experience in the workplace is more positive. In the private sector, they constitute a tiny minority within the expatriate-dominated workplace and often experience considerable alienation both from coworkers and from management.[41] Many find they are snubbed and experience comments such as "What are you doing here? You don't need the money." Such attitudes on the part of expatriate workers reflect the concern of many of them that localization policies signal that their jobs are under threat from locals.

To further explain the ostracizing of local workers and attempts to prevent them from integrating within the organization, we can refer to Byrne's Similarity Attraction Paradigm. This theory claims that people who see themselves as similar to each other will be more prone to like each other and become allies.[42] Frequently, expatriate employees fail to identify with local coworkers since they view them as very different from themselves. Expatriate workers often engage in tactics of alienation such as withholding information, thus diminishing the integration of local workers into the workplace. For example, many locals describe experiences of their expatriate colleagues preferring to do a task rather than explaining how it is done to a new local recruit. Such behaviors make it difficult for locals to learn the job and develop a useful role within the company, thus allowing foreign workers to maintain a competitive edge and ensuring their own survival within the company. The resulting sense of alienation leads to a high number of locals resigning from private sector positions.[43]

Managerial Communication Within Diverse Workforces

In summary, we can identify the following two major communication challenges that managers in the Gulf face:

1. The enormous cultural diversity that is likely to exist within their workforce. Managers need be sensitive to the often vastly different communication styles preferred by the cultures from which their workers originate and strive to succeed in interacting effectively with these culturally diverse groups.
2. The frequent rift between expatriate and local workers. Managers must be responsive to the often negative attitudes and behaviors of expatriate workers toward local workers.

An additional complication managers deal with is the common practice of using communication as a carpet under which to sweep bad behavior. For example, problems deriving from employees failing to carry out instructions or performing tasks properly are often glossed over with the excuse that there has been a "communication" problem. Gross rudeness is often explained away as "some miscommunication" between the persons concerned. This tactic helps to save face, that is, to avoid embarrassment for everyone involved; as we will discuss in Chapter 3, saving face is extremely important in Arab and Asian cultures. However, ignoring such issues does not serve to eradicate poor communication behavior or to identify the issues underlying the conflict or inefficiency. Managers will need to probe further into these so-called miscommunications to identify the real causes.

For a company to be able to operate effectively, a framework of organizational communication must exist to which all employees are able to adapt. That is, there must be a communication system in place that can accommodate differences and allow each employee to interact in a supportive and effective manner. The chapters that follow explore workplace communication and offer strategies for developing and implementing effective cross-cultural communication, including real-world business cases to help managers to develop the skills they need to navigate the communication conundrum that is inherent in the Gulf workplace.

CHAPTER 2

Culture in the Gulf

Culture is the collective programming of the mind which distinguishes the members of one category of people from another.[1]

Many managers in today's globalized business world will already have some sense of the impact of culture on attitudes and behavior. Their experience will have taught them that communication and other forms of behavior can vary considerably from that used in their own cultural context. Managers working with foreign nationals may observe, for instance, that negotiating and trouble-shooting can be approached in ways that are alien from their own natural response.

The Gulf context provides an additional challenge, in that expatriate employees in general can act and speak in ways very different from local employees working in the same organizations. These differences result from people's assumptions that stem from the cultural values instilled in them and by the behavioral norms sanctioned or prohibited within the cultures in which they were raised. The difference in these basic assumptions, and therefore what is or isn't considered to be acceptable behavior, results from the various ways certain cultures choose to solve the problems associated with organizing a society. These societal decisions include how power is distributed, the roles that groups and individuals should take, the value that should be attributed to ambition and caring for others, and the importance of rules and regulations. We will discuss each of these issues in this chapter.

Some elements of cultural differences are easy to recognize. These include such things as varying ways of dressing and eating, divergent styles of art, dancing, and other creative pursuits, and the observation of different holidays. However, many cultural differences are less visible and easy to overlook until they give rise to some kind of conflict or misunderstanding. These elements include such things as how people view the self, friendships, the differences between the genders and generations, and conceptions of justice, competition, cleanliness, and death. Indeed it is these hidden elements of culture that are actually most important in terms of beliefs, behavior, interaction, and communication.

A Framework for Looking at Culture

Although analyzing any culture in depth can be challenging, a comprehensive framework devised by Dutch social psychologist Geert Hofstede offers help in doing so. Hofstede's analysis is one of the best-known macro-theories of culture, taking into account the main differences that exist between cultures.[2]

Hofstede's research spanning more than 50 years began with a study he conducted when he was employed by IBM. In that initial study, he surveyed the values of IBM employees in over 50 countries. Since then, he and his research team have continued to collect extensive amounts of data from additional countries, with data now available for more than 100 different national cultures.[3] Hofstede's original framework consisted of four cultural dimensions taken from cultural anthropology, with a fifth dimension later added as a result of data collected on Asian cultures, and a sixth dimension most recently added as a result of further research.

Hofstede's six cultural dimensions, or scales, allow for a description of cultural patterns that can help us to investigate, describe, and then understand the influence of cultural differences in multicultural interactions. Based on responses to Hofstede's survey, each country is assigned a score from 1 to 100 for each dimension, and the score indicates the dominance of the particular trait within a given culture. For example, if a culture scores 90 on the cultural dimension that reflects the importance of individuals (Individualism), and another culture scores only 10, we can understand that the first culture is much more likely than the second culture to consider the rights of the individual. A description of each of Hofstede's cultural dimensions follows.

Power Distance

We can define power distance as the degree to which the less powerful members of any organization or community accept an unequal distribution of power and are willing to consent unquestioningly to the authority of those above them on the hierarchy.[4] In countries with high power distance, such as the Philippines, France, and the Arab countries, people will take for granted that the person above them in the hierarchy can control them, and they will tend to accept such control without question. In countries with low power distance, such as the Scandinavian nations, the United Kingdom, and the United States, people consider it necessary to have a more equal distribution of power.

Individualism Versus Collectivism

Collectivism is the degree to which individuals are integrated into groups. In more individualistic cultures, ties between people tend to be less binding and people are expected to take care of themselves and their own immediate families. Collectivist cultures, on the other hand, integrate individuals into groups, starting with the extended family, and individuals must display total loyalty to the group in return for continued protection.[5] More individualist cultures, such as the United States, Australia, and the United Kingdom, place greater value on individual rights and personal achievements. More collectivist countries, such as Indonesia, Thailand, and Korea, require people to place the group, whether this is family, community, organization, or nation, before the individual.

Uncertainty Avoidance

Uncertainty avoidance refers to a society's tolerance for ambiguity and reflects the degree to which a society's members will tolerate uncertainty and a lack of structure. Uncertainty avoiding cultures attempt to avoid unstructured situations by imposing strict codes of behavior and rules, by discouraging opinion and behavior that diverges from what is laid down as correct, and by encouraging the belief that an absolute truth can be applied to each and every situation.[6] Examples of countries with high uncertainly avoidance, and therefore a low tolerance of risk, include Greece, Portugal, and Belgium. In contrast, people in low uncertainty cultures feel comfortable with unknown situations and prefer to have fewer rules and regulations governing situations. Sweden, India, Singapore, and the United Kingdom are all examples of low uncertainty cultures that display a relatively high tolerance of risk.

Masculinity Versus Femininity

This dimension refers to how a society views pursuing ambition and the attainment of success compared to caring for the individuals within a society.[7] The term "masculine culture" is used to refer to societies such as Japan, the United States, and Italy that prize competitiveness, achievement, ambition, and power—characteristics typically ascribed to males. Common traits of such cultures include significant differentiation between gender roles, the dominance of men in leadership roles, and the obligation for men to be assertive and ambitious. Women who achieve leadership positions in such cultures may also need to be assertive and ambitious in order to be successful, and other women may be ambitious on behalf of the male members of their family, such as their husbands or sons. In such cultures, people will often live to work in order to achieve success and their professional ambitions, rather than working to live.

"Feminine culture," on the other hand, is the term used to refer to those cultures that prioritize quality of life, caring for others, and relationships between people—characteristics typically associated with females. In such cultures, gender roles are more diversified, people consider that family and work commitments should be balanced, sympathy for the weak is prized, and many women hold political and leadership roles. Examples of feminine cultures include Scandinavia, Canada, and the Netherlands. Given that Hofstede's choice of the masculine and feminine terms underscores the traditional role of men as ambitious and women as caring, some scholars have replaced the terms for this dimension with "quantity of life" (masculine) versus "quality of life" (feminine).

Long-Term Orientation

This dimension refers to how concerned cultures are with the past, present, and future. Long-term orientation societies tend to focus more on future achievement, perseverance, thrift, classifying the members of a society in terms of their status, and associating certain situations with an acute sense of shame. Short-term cultures, on the other hand, tend to focus on the present while maintaining a keen respect for tradition, social obligations, preserving "face," and personal stability.[8] Far Eastern countries such as China, Hong Kong, Taiwan, and Japan display long-term orientation while Nigeria, the Philippines, Norway, the United States, and the United Kingdom display short-term orientation.

Indulgence Versus Restraint

Indulgence refers to a culture's tendency to permit a fairly unrestricted fulfillment of the basic human desires for fun and enjoyment of life, while restraint refers to a cultural mindset that is wary of personal gratification of needs and regulates behavior by imposing rules.[9] Latin America, the United States, and the Nordic countries are examples of indulgent countries, whereas some Muslim countries, the Far East, and Eastern Europe represent restrained cultures.

Cultural Traits in the Gulf

Managers from other countries will find that they need to become more aware of their own culturally determined assumptions since many features of Gulf culture may vary considerably from that of the their home countries. Using Hofstede's framework, we will now look specifically at some of the cultural trends that are found in the Gulf and explore how these compare to Western cultures. Our discussion will focus on the implications that these differences have for workforce relations and communication.

High Power Distance

The GCC countries display high power distance, with Saudi Arabia and the UAE both scoring 80 as measured by Hofstede's framework. This is a much higher score than those of many Western countries, such as Austria (11), Denmark (18), Ireland (28), Norway and Sweden (31), the United Kingdom (35), and the United States (40). Not only do the local populations display high power distance, but the countries from which the majority of expatriate workers originate also rank high in terms of their unquestioning acceptance of authority. For example, the Philippines has a score of 94, Egypt and Iraq, 80, and India and Nigeria, 77.

This power distance trait plays a crucial role in how employees view managers, carry out their duties, and expect to be treated by management. Managers accustomed to their employees interacting with them as equals, offering feedback and suggestions, and perhaps questioning managerial decisions, will find that the typical workforce in the Gulf is far more compliant and ready to assume they will be given directions that are to be followed to the letter. Managers who think they are empowering workers by giving them greater control may, in fact, find their workers confused and disorientated by a lack of clear and authoritarian direction. Subordinates from high power distance cultures normally expect to be told what to do rather than to be consulted, and they typically respect those who display a strongly controlling approach.

Low Individualism

All the Gulf countries represent highly collectivist societies; Saudi Arabia, Kuwait, and the UAE all score 25 on the dimension of individualism. In comparison, the United States scores 91. The dominance of this cultural trait means that, once formed, groups tend to remain stable; and members of the same group are quick to offer each other help.[10] This willingness to help each other is strengthened by the fact that, as collectivists, a slur against one member of a group is considered as a slur against the entire group, so defense or protection of a member of one's own group is readily offered.[11]

Part of this tendency to ensure group stability is that members strive to maintain harmonious ways of interacting with each other, and they therefore tend to downplay anything that may be seen as a source of conflict or tension. Another aspect of this cultural trait is that Middle Easterners typically prefer to conduct interactions with people they know and with whom they have developed a relationship of trust.[12] We will discuss the importance of relationship building in more detail in Chapter 3.

Given the importance of trust and emphasis on the group, managers will find they have far more success in executing a task when some personal connection has already been established. This behavior differs from that of more individualist cultures where people tend to deal with the individual and the task at hand rather than considering the group to which the individual belongs. So managers may find that they often have to deal not just with the issue or the individual in front of them, but must also take into account the web of connections and history relating to the individual or task. For a person from a more task-focused, individualist culture, this approach can require some patience since it will seem to involve so many apparently irrelevant details.

High Uncertainty Avoidance

In the Gulf cultures, as in many Eastern cultures, uncertainty is viewed as a threat and differences from the norm tend not to be tolerated. The scores on uncertainty avoidance for the countries in the region are amongst the highest in the world, for example, Kuwait, Saudi Arabia, and the UAE all score 80 on this dimension (compared to 46 for the United States). Uncertainty and confusion are seen as sources of stress rather than being accepted as a part of life. The response to this is to regulate as much as possible in order to be able to govern all possible situations.

Managers, especially those from Northern European countries, may be surprised by the abundance of regulations and bureaucratic procedures that govern living and working in the Gulf. Endorsement and stamping of official documents, regulations governing entry to and exit from the various countries, and signing of documents all along the hierarchy, even for what one may consider trivial matters, are practices characteristic of a bureaucracy that must be accommodated.

The tendency to create complex bureaucracies in the attempt to avoid uncertainty is documented in the *Global Competitiveness Report* that identified inefficient bureaucracy as among the most problematic features of doing business in all the GCC countries.[13] Hofstede describes high uncertainty avoidance cultures as having "an emotional need for rules—even if not obeyed,"[14] and managers should be conscious of the many rules that exist and the complex bureaucracy that results.

High Masculinity

Only three Gulf countries have been investigated by Hofstede for the masculinity/femininity cultural trait. The UAE ranks midway (50) on this dimension indicating that it values competitiveness and success to the same degree that it values quality of life and caring for others. Saudi Arabia (60) displays greater masculinity, and therefore a greater interest in success and ambition, while Kuwait (40) displays less.

Again, the home countries of many Gulf expatriate workers display scores that fall either in the middle of the masculinity/femininity dimension or toward the higher end of the scale: Iraq (70), Philippines (64), India (56), Bangladesh (55), Syria (52), Pakistan (50), and, Egypt and Jordan (45). In the case of Iraq and the Philippines, for instance, this high masculinity score indicates the presence of strong competitiveness, maximum differentiation between genders, the view that men should be assertive and ambitious, as well as an admiration for strength. This is in stark contrast to the cultural tendencies of the Nordic countries, the Netherlands, and the Latin countries, all of which score at the bottom end of the scale (e.g., Sweden is at 5). Managers from such femininity-oriented countries may find it challenging to work with or manage people from cultures that are considerably more masculine than their own.

Long-Term Versus Short-Term Orientation

Saudi Arabia is the only country in the Gulf where the long-term versus short-term orientation dimension has been investigated by the Hofstede team. A relatively low score of 36 on this dimension means that Saudi nationals consider the past as sacrosanct, do not like societal change, generally do not plan for the future, and focus on the short term rather than the long term. Although data for other Gulf countries is not yet available, the cultural similarities between them on most of the other dimensions (apart from the masculinity–femininity dimension) would suggest that they are likely to share a similar short-term orientation.

Most of the other cultures that make up the diverse workforce in the GCC also have a short-term leaning, for example, Jordan (16), Lebanon (14), and the Philippines (26). As a result, for managers from countries such as the United States (26) and Canada (36), the impact of this cultural trait may cause fewer difficulties than some of the other dimensions we have discussed because of the relative similarities between their cultures and that of their employees. There are two notable exceptions, however; India has a score of 51 and Russia an extremely high score of 81, indicating a strong long-term orientation. Employees from these countries tend to be happy to consider change and look to the future rather than to the past.

Balanced Indulgence Versus Restraint

Finally, on the indulgence versus restraint dimension, again only Saudi Arabia has been investigated and it has a mid-range score of 52.[15] According to Hofstede's analysis, Saudi Arabia, and, we might assume, the other Gulf nations, is neither an indulgent (hedonistic) or restrained (controlled) culture. Some of the other major groups working in the region show much lower scores, for example, India scores 26, Russia, 20, Lebanon, 25, and the Philippines, 42. This suggests that people from these cultures place less emphasis on leisure time and having fun than is likely to be the case for their counterparts from countries such as the United States (68), Denmark (70), and Australia (71). Managers from Western countries may find that their Gulf region employees appear to take life more seriously than they do.

Further Points on Gulf Culture

Cultural Perspectives on Time

The way in which cultures think about time has been described by scholars as falling into one of two perspectives referred to as monochronic and polychronic.[16] Monochronic cultures view time as linear, they tend to make and adhere strictly to schedules, and they prefer to move sequentially from one task to another. Polychronic cultures, on the other hand, see time as cyclical, are given to multitasking, and do not view time as a limited resource. For managers from monochronic cultures such as North America and Northern Europe, it is important to bear this distinction in mind. The Gulf represents a polychronic culture and its people view multitasking as acceptable so during a meeting, for instance, they may engage in other activities such as answering a phone call or handling a question from an employee who is otherwise not involved in the meeting. Managers from monochronic cultures may at first find this disconcerting as they will prefer to focus on one task at a time in a linear way and are less likely to be tolerant of interruptions.

Punctuality does not have the same value in polychronic cultures as it does in monochronic cultures. As a result, managers from monochronic cultures may have to deal with what appears to them to be delayed starts and last-minute changes to schedules. On the other hand, Gulf Arabs, with their polychronic approach to time, will find it difficult to understand why their monochronic business partners object to a change in schedule, and they will view this as a sign of inflexibility.

Islam

When discussing culture in the Gulf, it is impossible not to mention the role played by religion. Islam is the religion of almost all Gulf nationals, and it has a pervasive influence on their lifestyles. It also has an influence on the way in which business is conducted in the region.

The Islamic day of rest is Friday, and throughout the GCC the weekend comprises Friday and Saturday. Government offices are closed on Friday, and the most important religious point in the day is during the time of the third prayer, beginning just after noon. During Ramadan, the month of fasting and special prayer, the pattern of life changes a great deal. The working day is typically shortened; there is no need for a lunch break as Muslims are required to fast from sunrise till sunset. Managers will need to be particularly careful in their expectations at this time since many members of their workforce will be fasting and perhaps unable to work at their normal standard of performance. Fasting is enforced by law and everyone, Muslim and non-Muslim alike, is forbidden from eating in public. Although rare, breaking the ban on fasting in public during daylight hours, can potentially lead to arrest or to problems with the authorities. Drinking, chewing gum, and smoking are also banned in public places, and it is considered insensitive to draw attention to eating and drinking during this time. Most workplaces set aside a designated area in which non-Muslims may eat and drink, and hotel restaurants remain open but may be screened off from public view.

Islam forbids Muslims from consuming alcohol. However, with the exception of Saudi Arabia, Kuwait, and the Emirate of Sharjah in the UAE, alcohol is available for purchase by non-Muslims in specially licensed stores and for consumption in bars, hotels, and restaurants throughout the Gulf. There is, however, a certain opposition to the sale of alcohol among some locals in the Gulf,[17] and it is always best to treat the issue of alcohol delicately and avoid referring to it openly. That is, while Gulf Arabs are typically tolerant of different ways of life, they will not appreciate being exposed to things that are considered to be unacceptable within Islam.

Haram is the Arabic word for forbidden or not good, and its opposite is *halal*, meaning good or acceptable. The consumption of food items, most notably pork, is *haram*; and although pork is available for non-Muslims in some countries in the region, non-Muslims should avoid talking about it in conversation with Muslims. In general, visitors from outside of the region should remember that Muslims tend to place great importance on the issue of what is *haram* and *halal* both in terms of consumption and of personal care.[18]

Another aspect of Islamic principles is the prescription of modesty in dress. In Saudi Arabia, for instance, all women are required to wear an *abaya* in public, that is, a long, loose, lightweight black coat, and ideally they should also cover their heads with the *shayla* (a long chiffon head-scarf). In other parts of the Gulf, this is unnecessary for foreign women, but they should cover their knees and their upper arms. Men should also dress relatively formally for work purposes since conservative dress is appreciated. It is worth remembering that many people in the region consider it shameful not to dress respectably, most especially for professional purposes. This is particularly true during the month of Ramadan when Muslims are more focused on religion and conservatism is more pronounced.

Arabic in the Gulf

Gulf Arabic, also referred to as *Khaliji* Arabic, is the version of Arabic that is spoken in Eastern Arabia around the coast of the Gulf. While Saudi Arabia has its own distinct dialect (Saudi Arabic), the dialects of the other Gulf countries share many similarities. In Bahrain, the Sunni dialect is considered by many people to be a prestigious form of local Arabic, but in general, a homogeneous Gulf Arabic is shared across the region.[19] Apart from its value as the native language of Gulf Arabs, Arabic enjoys a high status given that it is the language of the *Koran* and religious rites.

It should be noted that, despite the diversity of language use throughout the Gulf and the dominance of English as the language of business, Gulf Arabs will appreciate indications of respect for their language such as when foreigners are familiar with some Arabic words and have their business cards printed in Arabic as well as English. A common greeting for Muslims is "assalamu alaikum" meaning "peace be with you" and the response is "wa alaikum assalam," meaning "peace be upon you, too." Because Arabic is the official language of all GCC countries, all formal documents such as contracts must be translated into Arabic.

Wasta—The Underlying Power of Personal Connection

Given the collectivist culture of the region and the importance of relationships of trust, personal connections are highly valued. Having a personal relationship with an individual implies a willingness to consider the person a potential ally as well as a person who should be helped in times of need. Such understanding of mutual assistance and support is a powerful dynamic and exerts a major impact on how business and social relations are conducted throughout the Arab world.[20] In Arabic this practice is termed *wasta*, which can be regarded as roughly equivalent to the English expression "It's not what you know, but who you know."

The concept and practice of *wasta* is so common that the word has crept into U.S. military circles as a result of U.S. military presence in the Middle East.[21] In the Gulf it is sometimes referred to as "vitamin W." It operates in an analogous way to similar networks of alliances in other cultural contexts such as, for instance, what is often referred to as the "old boys" networks in the United States and the United Kingdom. *Wasta* can have far reaching consequences, and managers may find that they need to alter their behavior toward a particular person on the basis that he or she has *wasta*, that is, a high level of influence with some key stakeholder.

Wasta has been described by some as having a negative impact on companies in situations in which an individual may be recruited or promoted on the basis of personal connections rather than ability alone.[22]

Traditionally young men in the GCC countries were reluctant to apply for a position in the normal way as it indicated they did not have the *wasta*, that is, the connections within the community, to secure a job. However, this has changed in recent times and it has become more common to apply for positions in the normal way.[23] However, *wasta* can also operate in a positive way when personal connections may help solve problems and expedite procedures. That is, a personal connection may serve to establish a company's or an individual's reliability and trustworthiness, thus dispensing with a usual lengthy protocol.

While some view *wasta* as essentially cronyism or nepotism, it originates from a collectivist desire to offer help to members of one's circle. It is therefore a reflection of a code of honor that requires the extension of assistance to others. This historical code of mutual help stems from the harsh desert conditions that rendered the granting of help to others of paramount importance.[24] However it manifests itself in business, it is useful for managers to be aware of the dynamic underlying it and to handle it sensitively.

CHAPTER 3

Communication in the Gulf

The strength of a person is in his intelligence and his tongue.
—Arabic Proverb

People who travel to different parts of the world often notice that the way they do things is very different from the behavior of people in the country they are visiting. A simple illustration of such differences can be seen when North Americans visiting Greece are surprised by the fact that it is "culturally allowed" to slightly push others out of the way in crowded situations. In the United States, this would be considered offensive. Differences such as these are embedded in what is referred to as the distinction between high context and low context cultures. Greece is a high context culture in which a gentle push would be an acceptable nonverbal equivalent of the words "Please allow me to pass." In North America, a low context culture, people would expect the polite verbal request and would not be able to appropriately process the nonverbal message of pushing.

In this chapter we focus on features of Gulf communication that may perplex new managers, especially those of Western origin. The distinction between high context versus low context cultures and the impact of this dimension on preferred communication styles provides a useful way of doing this.

Context—High Context and Low Context Cultures

The North American cultural anthropologist Edward Hall described the notion of high context and low context communication as follows:

> A high context (HC) communication or message is one in which most of the information is either in the physical context or internalized in the person, while very little is in the coded, explicit,

transmitted part of the message. A low context (LC) communication is just the opposite; i.e., the mass of the information is vested in the explicit code.[1]

Hall also elaborated on differences between high context and low context cultures and their communication characteristics.[2] The most significant features of communication in high context cultures can be described as follows:

- High context cultures rely heavily on nonverbal elements such as facial expression, eye movement, and tone of voice to convey meaning.
- The context in which the communication takes place and the relationships between the people involved are of great importance.
- Less importance is placed on the words, and often the true meaning of a message lies in how it is said rather than in the actual meaning of the words used. For example, a polite response such as "Yes, of course, I will help you," may be said in a vague way and the real message would be understood as "I most probably won't help you."

In low context cultures, communication is characterized as follows:

- The words used generally have greater significance than any accompanying body language.
- Messages are ideally expressed in a concise, direct, and explicit way.
- The task or goal of a discussion is given greater importance than the relationships between the persons involved.

Hall suggests that the difference in the preferred styles of communication of high context and low context societies is perhaps one of the greatest differences between the Eastern and Western worlds. This difference can certainly cause difficulties in work-related discussions when people from both high context and low context cultures are involved, as many of their communication strategies are diametrically opposed to each other. This means, for instance, that when people from the Gulf, a high context culture, are working with people from the United States, Germany, or the United Kingdom, all of which are low context cultures, the ways they approach a discussion will be very different.[3]

Arab cultures in general are considered to be high context cultures, and they place great importance on the context of the communication. Context essentially refers to "how much you have to know before effective communication can occur; how much shared knowledge is taken for granted by those in conversation with each other; how much reference there is to tacit common ground."[4] Gulf Arabs communicate with each other largely on the basis of a pre-existing shared understanding, and foreign managers need to be conscious of this since they will not necessarily be familiar with all the undercurrents and nuances that are readily apparent to a local person.

Establishing a Relationship Before Starting a Discussion

Establishing a personal relationship in order to develop trust is an essential prerequisite for any successful interaction in the Gulf. Gulf Arabs like to know a good deal about the other person's context before they can really communicate with him or her. This personal connection and the trust implied in it, recreates the conditions to which Gulf Arabs are accustomed and need when conducting a meaningful conversation. Building trust often starts with small talk that helps develop interpersonal relationships. This small talk is not typically related to personal aspects of an individual's life; indeed, such personal information is generally considered private and not appropriate in general conversation. Instead, sharing cultural interests or commonly accepted facts known to both parties can be a noncontroversial way of letting Gulf Arabs know more about yourself. General topics such as food, traditions, everyday habits, or the general business context in which both parties are working are generally not threatening to commonly shared values and can contribute to relationship building. The British linguist Brigitte Planken has referred to such topics as "safe talk," that is useful for the creation of rapport, which is of paramount importance in the Gulf.[5]

Some Points About Arabic Communication

Arabic has a rich oral tradition in which creative metaphors, analogies, and story telling all play an important role.[6] A focus on grandeur in verbal expression means that Arabic is viewed as "an art form, a religious phenomenon, and an identity tool."[7]

Arabic speaking style tends to be holistic and circular rather than discrete or linear: "Instead of presenting a case by building an argument point by point, the Arabic speaker tends to present the whole picture. The end result. The catastrophe. The victory."[8] Given that the persuasive power of discourse lies in the presentation of the idea itself and not in its proof, emotions play an important role in Arabic rhetoric.[9] This means that Arabs will often aim to "speak to the heart" of the listener. This does not mean, however, that Arabs readily display their emotions in their everyday interactions. Indeed, many Gulf Arabs tend to be very conservative in showing their emotions in public arenas.

Repetition, which we will talk about more in Chapter 5, is a notable feature of the narrative quality of Arabic discourse.[10] Another important characteristic is that speakers tend to discuss things in a nonlinear way, that is, they do not necessarily proceed from a single point to another single point. Moreover, given that Arabs are high context people, they often support what they say with nonverbal signs and implicit messages such as, for instance, a facial expression or particular tone of voice.[11]

The great focus that high context societies place on the context of the message or discussion can present challenges when Arabs need to write, rather than talk about, a message, especially in formal situations. This is because in written messages many of the necessary contextual cues are absent. Moreover, when the highly contextualized nature of Arabic speech is subjected to different cultural standards of logic or persuasion, the contrast becomes even more evident. This dilemma has been observed in English language classrooms where it has frequently been noted that Arab students who have superb essay writing skills in Arabic may construct essays in English that would be viewed as out of focus by native English speakers.[12]

The Prominence of Honor in Gulf Communication

Throughout the Gulf there is a strong tendency to work to preserve one's personal honor. This means that it is customary to place more emphasis on the emotional work of protecting one's honor and that of other participants in the interaction than on the cognitive work that is inherent in a discussion. While a Western person may be totally focused on the meaning and implications of a message—the cognitive element—the Gulf Arab will also focus on the impact of the message on the people involved in the discussion. This tendency is illustrated by a study comparing Qataris with those from the United States. It found that Qataris, members of an honor culture, shared less information in their discussion than did the Americans. The Americans, on the other hand, displayed more competitiveness, ambition, and stronger negative emotions in their speech. This is a significant point of difference as any show of competitiveness or negative response could be interpreted by Gulf nationals as threatening the honor of the people involved in the discussion.[13]

The issue of honor is pervasive in Gulf society. It represents a secular rather than a religious value, and family structure is mainly preserved through honor.[14] In multicultural work contexts, it is important to understand the role that honor plays in determining what people will be comfortable talking about and how they conduct themselves. One important point is that a male visitor to the region should never ask male Arabs about their female family members, as this may be viewed as a threat to the family's honor. Women, however, may more freely ask other women questions. Another important aspect of honor relates to a person's word. A handshake in agreement means much more than a written contract, and the oral contract it implies is seen as binding.

Saving Face and "Facework"

In high context societies, people are often silent about their feelings and thoughts.[15] Their messages tend to be indirect and subtle, and one has to "read between the lines" in order to understand the true meaning behind the words. The main reason high context individuals are often ambiguous and cautious in what they say is because they want to "save face," that is, they do not want to cause embarrassment to others or to themselves. *Face* is defined "as the positive social value a person effectively claims for himself by the line others assume he has taken during a particular contact."[16] While the issue of face features in all cultures,[17] it has considerable importance in collectivist cultures like those in the Gulf. This is because "collectivists tend to have an interdependent view of the self, which fosters a sensitivity to the needs of others and, at the same time, a need for sensitivity from others."[18] This notion of face plays a role both in gaining trust and in maintaining honor, and concern for face is very evident in how Gulf people conduct their interpersonal relationships.

In order to maintain the trust that is so important in relationships, Gulf Arabs will be careful to treat others with dignity and respect so that no one involved in the interaction will be threatened by a loss of face. This means that their communication style tends to be characterized by patience, self-control, and a willingness to compromise.[19] In order to avoid face-threatening situations, Arabs carry out what is known as *facework*. While all cultures use facework to a greater or lesser degree, it is of particular importance for high context cultures that place considerable value on maintaining relationships. This concern for face may generate a different dynamic in discussions than normally would be the case in low context cultures. For example, Gulf people will be more inclined to indicate agreement when they don't actually agree in order to not cause offence, or they will choose to avoid the topic altogether. To illustrate this, in a study comparing UK and Gulf nationals, it was observed that "in fear of losing face and in a desire to remain humble, Arabs are more likely to ignore something they disagree with, than openly reject or criticise it."[20]

Face and the Avoidance of Uncertainty

Face is also related to Hofstede's cultural dimension of uncertainty avoidance that we discussed in Chapter 2, and which refers to "the level of stress in a society in the face of an unknown future."[21] Uncertainty avoiding cultures, such as those of the Gulf, try to minimize unknown or unstructured situations by developing strict rules to govern their behaviors. The more a culture tends to avoid uncertainty, the more likely it is to engage in facework, and this is particularly true of Arab cultures. Arabs employ numerous ritualistic facework strategies, that is, repetitive actions that tend to create predictability in interactions. By using such rituals and hence generating greater predictability within the conversation, it is easier to maintain face as the element of the unknown is reduced and people are better prepared to effectively handle each stage of the communication. Given the importance of facework and verbal rituals that this implies, it is generally not effective for managers to adopt a more casual approach to conversation that is common in low context cultures.

Another example of how the cultural trend of reducing uncertainty is managed is the commonly used expression "Inshallah," which means, "God willing." Some people interpret this expression as being used to downplay personal responsibility in a given matter and leaving things to chance rather than taking specific action. However, its common use actually originates in the need to reduce uncertainty and to ensure a sense of security by leaving things in the control of a greater power. It also serves to keep communication open and positive as it acts as a safety valve. That is, any failure to keep a promise or carry out an action will not be attributed to a personal reluctance on the part of the speaker, which might otherwise cause that person and the people interacting with them to lose face.

Face Versus Honor

Although for the Gulf Arab both face and honor play a role in communication, honor is generally given more importance than face. On the one hand, the preservation of face means that Gulf people will seek to preserve harmony in their interactions. On the other hand, the high value placed on honor can lead people to act assertively, and sometimes aggressively, in the face of conflict. While Gulf people prefer to act politely and appreciate high levels of civility from the people they encounter in working environments, their sense of honor is crucial. It is, therefore, essential to avoid risking damage to a person's sense of honor. For managers from other parts of the world, it is advisable to be formal, to try to understand and follow the communication rituals that exist, and to be conscious of the multiple aims of reducing uncertainty, saving face, and preserving honor.

Oral Versus Written Agreements

As mentioned earlier in this chapter, people from high context societies consider a handshake or a spoken agreement as binding. Conversely, low context societies place more importance on the written contract. For low context societies, the written word is binding, while for high context societies it often is not. As a result, among Gulf Arabs "contracts are viewed as memorandums of understanding rather than binding, fixed agreements."[22] This important distinction changes the emphasis that is placed on a written business contract. That is, while people from low context societies seek clarity and detail in a written business contract, high context societies require less detail and are more comfortable if the text is open to interpretation. This difference in emphasis on written agreements should be understood by both parties and would need to be thoroughly discussed between the high context and low context participants in any business arrangement.

Nonverbal Communication

In contrast to their low context counterparts, high context societies don't just listen to the words that are being spoken; they place great emphasis on the other features involved in the communication. This means that nonverbal communication is extremely important for high context individuals, and they use nonverbal communication extensively to enhance their intended meaning. For example, while a high context speaker may use positive-sounding words with little conviction to signal a rejection in a nonthreatening way, the same words may sound overtly positive to a low context listener who is not accustomed to listening for additional clues as to what the speaker really means. The real and significant meaning of such an interaction should be recognized as a negative message, a "no," that is being expressed obliquely rather than directly in order to preserve the speakers' face. The physical cues, that is, the nonverbal element of the communication, play a major role in how the message is formulated and meant to be understood.

Nonverbal communication tends to play a much more minor role in low context cultures; this means that people from low context societies must develop a keener sensitivity to the nonverbal elements of a message that is being conveyed by a Gulf Arab or any person from a high context culture.

Touch

The issue of touch is very important in nonverbal communication as touch, or the absence of it, plays a significant role in how we communicate. For example, shaking hands to many throughout the world indicates a willingness to interact with each other, or it functions as a sign of agreement. In the Gulf, however, touching is only acceptable between family members and, in the case of nonfamily members, between people of the same sex. Even in emergency situations, such as accidents and in hospitals, touching the opposite sex is considered offensive.[23]

When dealing with females from the Gulf, the issue of touch is particularly sensitive. Because of the strong proscription against any form of contact between unrelated males and females, males should be particularly wary of making any physical contact with a Gulf female. In general, for instance, a man should not offer his hand to a Gulf woman. This can lead to embarrassment, although many Gulf women will respond graciously by not offering their hand but instead placing it across their heart in a sign of friendship. This response is a means of saving face in that the woman physically expresses her commitment to friendly discussion while signaling her discomfort with any form of physical contact with an unrelated man.

Personal Space

Another important element of nonverbal communication is the issue of personal space. We are all culturally influenced by how much personal space we need to feel comfortable while in conversation with others. Studies of the degree of personal space expected within different cultures reveals that North Americans typically like to have a great deal of space around them, while people from Southern Mediterranean cultures prefer less, and Arabs tend to feel comfortable with even less.[24] These differences need to be kept in mind when trying to establish a comfortable arrangement for a discussion. A commonly told story is that of a businessman from the United States in discussion with an Arab businessman. The Arab man, feeling uncomfortable with too much physical gap between himself and his counterpart, moves closer to the American. The American, preferring more personal space, moves away. A "dance" ensues as each moves toward or away from the other in the attempt to set up the physical environment with which he is most comfortable. It is therefore useful for foreign managers to closely observe what degree of physical space and contact seems appropriate for the other person.

But the Gulf Workforces Are Full of Non-Gulf People!

The well-known proverb "When in Rome, do as the Romans do" may be difficult to apply in the Gulf. This is because the vast majority of people working in the Gulf come from different parts of the world, and it may not be easy to know which "Romans" to imitate. This problem is complicated by the fact that in the Gulf, as in other high context cultures, it is common procedure to regulate behavior by correcting people individually and verbally rather than by written rules and signs. In high context cultures rules of behavior are implicit, well known, and shared among members of the group. Low context societies, on the other hand, tend to prefer to have formally established and openly publicized rules. Given this, it may be difficult for managers new to the region to clearly identify what kind of behavior is expected in a particular situation.

This situation of not knowing which model to follow is very different from that experienced in other countries with large numbers of expatriates in the workforce, such as Singapore. In Singapore, the local way of doing things dominates and expatriates are expected to adapt to this norm. In the Gulf, given that the local culture does not tend to dominate in workplace communication outside of the public sector, managers may find a range of informal, implicit codes in operation and perhaps struggle to find an appropriate cultural anchor around which to develop their management style.

CHAPTER 4

Intercultural Communication

Business English as a Lingua Franca (BELF) is a 'neutral' and shared communication code.[1]

In this chapter we move on from our examination of cultural differences to a discussion of intercultural communication and the ways in which people from the Gulf manage to communicate successfully with people from outside the Gulf. We will consider the languages that are used in the region, the strategies that people use to facilitate the numerous intercultural interactions that take place on a daily basis, and the achievement of what we will call "rapport" through the management of talk between people interacting in the workplace.

Business English as a Lingua Franca

The Dominance of English

One of the most important developments in the Gulf over the past 50 years has been the exponential increase in the use of English. Although globalization and expanded technology have influenced this trend in many other parts of the world, it is hard to imagine how the region could have developed in the way that it has without a willingness on the part of the local population to use English alongside Arabic. There is some variation across the region in how much English is used; it is used more, for instance, in the UAE and less in Saudi Arabia. However, English and Arabic tend to coexist quite easily, particularly for the younger, generally tech-savvy generation now entering the workforce.

Before the rapid development of the oil industry in the 1960s, much business in the region was conducted in Arabic, and the traders and merchants who visited the region generally used Arabic for business interactions. Even during the pre-oil era, however, there were some schools in the region that had begun to offer English, notably in Dubai. As the oil industry developed, engineers and other technical staff were brought into the region, often from the United States and other Western countries. As a result, English quickly replaced Arabic as the *de facto* lingua franca, not only in business, but also in other social domains.

English is often used in interactions between people who do not speak it as their first language to allow them to communicate and therefore carry out business and achieve their purposes. Urdu is much used in the construction and agricultural sectors in the region, and some expatriates, such as domestic staff and retail staff, continue to learn Arabic in order to find employment, most especially in Saudi Arabia. However, most observers agree that English now underpins many business related activities in the region. A survey carried out at the Dubai Police Department in 2010, showed that employees at all levels within the Dubai Police Force needed to be able to speak and understand English. Additionally, from 2015 onward, all taxi drivers in the Emirate of Dubai are tested on their English language skills (but not on their Arabic) before being offered employment.[2]

Arabic and English

Arabic dialects vary considerably across the Arabic-speaking world. As a result, communication may sometimes be difficult even between two Arabic speakers when they are from different regions, such as a Gulf Arab communicating with a Tunisian.

However, English is now so prevalent in some social contexts such as in retail and restaurants in the larger cities that residents often use it automatically regardless of who they are addressing.

Increasing numbers of Gulf children attend international schools, which means that their education takes place almost entirely in English from kindergarten onward. In addition, in recent years, there has also been a move toward the use of more English in government schools, and government and private universities across the region largely use English as their medium of instruction. The result of this trend has been that younger people in the Gulf often switch between English and Arabic throughout the course of their day, and some young families have also begun to speak English rather than Arabic with their children because they see this as an advantage. Young people may speak only Arabic at home with their parents and grandparents, for instance, but switch between the two languages with their friends and siblings, and then use only English in restaurants and while shopping. As a result, many Gulf nationals under the age of 30 are very used to living their lives through the medium of both Arabic and English.

Young women, especially as they are now very likely to complete tertiary education and advance rapidly through the lower ranks of employment, may have better English language skills than their male counterparts, and there is some evidence that young women in the region have a preference for English, whereas young men retain a preference for Arabic. Older businesspeople in particular, may not only speak Arabic and English, but also Hindi and Urdu.[3]

Despite the undeniable shift toward English as an important means of communication, there are mixed feelings in the region about this change. While many Gulf nationals from the large cities are pragmatic about English and accept its widespread use as a part of globalization and a facilitator of both economic and technological advancement, they are also aware that it poses a threat to Arabic and to their traditional way of life. For older people in particular, and most especially for older, Arabic-speaking women who have not generally participated in the workforce, the increasing reliance on English in nondomestic contexts has caused some sense of alienation in their own country. Local residents point to the fact that Arabic is the language of the Koran, and it is therefore a crucial element in their cultural heritage. As a result, efforts have been made in the past few years by governments to ensure that Arabic continues to be studied in schools and universities.

The extent to which English is officially tolerated varies to some degree across the region, for example, in Saudi Arabia brand names in English are translated into Arabic or phonetically transcribed into Arabic script, whereas they are frequently left in their original version in the

UAE. In summary, although English is widely accepted and used, it is also worth remembering as a visitor that there may be some sensitivity about the cultural and religious significance of Arabic.

As we have discussed, the multicultural nature of the larger cities in the region means that many of the interactions that take place are between two speakers who opt for English as a lingua franca. Research has shown that when it is used in this way, English is considered as both a shared and a neutral communication code.[4] This means that the people who use it to facilitate their interactions and get their work done do not associate it with any one of the nations in the world where the majority of the population happen to speak English as their first language. Having said that, however, TV shows, films, and even school curricula from both the United States and the United Kingdom are all commonly available across the region, with the exception of the national media channels in Saudi Arabia. This ready availability has prompted a continuing discussion in the media and within government about the importance of preserving Arabic and the culture associated with the language. Although people who work in government organizations such as ministries and other semigovernmental organizations may need more Arabic than English on a daily basis, those who opt to work in the private sector will deal with an expatriate-dominated workforce, and they therefore need to use English for a great number of their work interactions.

The Influence of English

For people coming to the region, the prevalence of English makes life easy to negotiate. Signage is generally bilingual, as is a great deal of advertising, and the retail, health, and education sectors all provide large numbers of employees with excellent English language skills. The large expatriate communities that exist across the region mean that a manager is less likely to be speaking to a Gulf local than to an employee from India, Pakistan, the Philippines, another part of the Middle East, or Europe. In business organizations, especially in the private sector, the relatively low numbers of local employees means that many, if not most, business interactions will take place between speakers from other parts of the world and not necessarily from the Gulf.

Accommodation in Interactions

One of the first people to talk about how speakers of different cultures accommodate each other in interactions was the U.S. professor Howard Giles. His Communication Accommodation Theory is centered on the idea that when people interact, they adjust their speech, vocal patterns, and gestures to accommodate to others.[5] Communication Accommodation Theory includes both verbal and nonverbal communication, and Giles suggests that speakers use two sets of strategies in their communication. These are convergence strategies focused on trying to reduce the differences between themselves and the other speaker and capitalize on the similarities, and divergence strategies that emphasize the differences between themselves and the person with whom they are interacting.

In using convergence, a speaker tries to increase the effectiveness of the communication by moving toward the way in which their counterpart uses language, for example, by replicating their pronunciation or their nonverbal communication. This can help to put the other speaker at ease. However, too much convergence can be viewed as over-accommodation and perceived as patronizing. In contrast, speakers may use divergence and accentuate the differences between themselves and the other person as a way of maintaining the identity and importance of the group to which each speaker belongs. Speakers who use divergence strategies can succeed in conveying a strong sense of their cultural and social identity and an appreciation and understanding of the other person's culture as well.

Elements of Communication Accommodation Theory can be useful for understanding the communication that takes place routinely between people from different cultures living in the Gulf. First is the fact that research has shown that in situations where nations are dependent on people from other countries, for example, in economies focused on tourism, the local population tends to accommodate and "converge" with the language strategies of the visiting population, rather than the other way around. The Gulf has not traditionally been dependent on tourism, although there has been some recent rapid development of the tourism industry. However, it has been heavily dependent on outside help for its economic and technological advancement. As a result, many locals are very familiar with dealing with non-Gulf people, and they generally accommodate to the other speaker through convergence. People visiting from outside the region will usually find that local residents are willing to accommodate to their communication. As we have discussed in previous chapters, however, the rules governing male–female interactions will always be more tightly controlled than interactions that do not involve both genders, especially in the observation of the non-touch rule between the genders. This is not only the case for Gulf Arabs compared to Western societies but also for many of the other major groups that live and work in the region, including Indians, Pakistanis, and those from other parts of the Middle East.

A second application of the Communication Accommodation Theory focuses on what happens in interactions between native and non-native speakers of a language. As we discussed earlier, many people who do not speak English as their first language nevertheless opt to use it as a lingua franca to communicate in the workplace. Research in accommodation shows that although English is viewed as a neutral, cultureless communication tool comparable to the tool of computer literacy, speakers are still likely to converge toward the norms of native English speakers when they are in conversation with them. On the other hand, some native speakers have a tendency to either over-accommodate and speak English, for example, in a way that is oversimplified and therefore patronizing to the other party, or they fail to accommodate at all to the needs of the non-native speaker and they therefore become incomprehensible.

More on Native Speakers and Non-Native Speakers

In the Gulf region, a huge variation exists in the prior experiences people have had with English, whether in school or university in the GCC or elsewhere in the world. This means that managers in the region are likely to be dealing with varying levels of language proficiency and fluency, often within the same organization or even within the same meeting. As one would expect, there is a great deal of variation in the array of English language skills that includes not only speaking, but also listening, reading, and writing.

Native speakers of English, in particular, may find that they need to accommodate other speakers, choose their words and expressions carefully, and slow down their rate of speech. Many managers may find that speakers of English from India speak much more quickly than they themselves do. Moreover, North American managers in particular may observe that there is much more tolerance for interruption and overlapping speech in the Gulf than there is in many other parts of the world. For instance, people from India, the United Kingdom, and Italy, routinely interrupt each other without a threat to face, that is, without appearing to be impolite. Likewise, speakers from high context cultures in general, such as India, Russia, and the Arab-speaking nations, will have a much greater tolerance for people conducting more than one conversation at the same time and also engaging in other tasks while involved in a conversation, than do people from the low context cultures of the West.

Even though everyone may be speaking English in a given workplace interaction, they are each also likely to transfer into the interaction the communication patterns and strategies that are characteristic of their own cultural background. Research on this phenomena has shown that people continue to prefer their own style of communication and the communication strategies they would use in their own first language, regardless of the fact that they are speaking English.[6] Again, for native English speakers in particular, this can be disconcerting. It is important to remember that lingua franca English has evolved into a neutral, cultureless, communication tool for many non-native business people; but such speakers may still transfer some of their own first-language communication style into their use of English.

Strategies for Success

The British linguist Pamela Rogerson-Revell provides some useful insights into how speakers can accommodate each other in intercultural business interactions.[7] Although her work was carried out in the context of meetings at the European Commission, the multicultural, and sometimes multilingual, nature of those meetings has relevance for the Gulf where meetings between speakers with different first languages and various cultural backgrounds are commonplace. Rogerson-Revell's research is particularly important because it addresses why people who do not speak English as their first language participate less than people who do. The non-native speakers in the study reported that they stayed silent because they felt they couldn't express themselves properly, and they also did not feel that they could interrupt someone else in an effective way. On the other hand, although the native speakers of English understood that it was important for them to accommodate the non-English speakers and modify their speech patterns, the non-native speakers reported that they didn't think that they often achieved this.

Rogerson-Revell's research also sheds light on how people experience being a part of a multicultural meeting, and it provides some strategies that can help make communication successful for all people involved. The analysis of successful multicultural meetings showed that speakers used several different strategies to put all participants at ease and move the communication forward. First of all, if participants did use incorrect or idiosyncratic English, others did not correct them as long as the message was comprehensible. On the other hand, when either native or non-native speakers used English in such a way that it wasn't easy to understand, the best communicators found a way to clarify with them what they had just said. Asking for clarification and checking for meaning were important ways of moving the communication toward a successful conclusion.

Other accommodation strategies were also noted in Rogerson-Revell's research that reflect Giles' convergence theory. For instance, speakers emphasized that common ground is created when everyone in the meeting carefully followed the procedural rules and waited for their turn to speak without interrupting. Native English speakers also modified their English by speaking slowly and clearly, with minimal use of idiomatic expressions. These strategies allowed the non-native participants to feel comfortable participating in the meeting and that they could understand what was being said around them. As we have noted, the different versions of English spoken in the Gulf coupled with varying levels of proficiency in the language mean that managers must continually seek to accommodate all members of their workforces.

Managing the Talk

The British linguist Helen Spencer Oatey has written extensively on what she refers to as the management of rapport as a major contributor to the success or failure of intercultural interactions, particularly in negotiations. Spencer-Oatey believes that the way that people manage the talk that takes place in a negotiation can either create or destroy a feeling of rapport between them. For people from high context cultures, such as many of the cultural groups who live and work in the Gulf region, finding common ground between people and creating a sense of rapport is a crucial step in building a business relationship and therefore facilitating working relations.[8]

Spencer-Oatey's research shows that people can manage the talk that takes place in a negotiation so that it contributes in a positive way to building the relationship between them; and, as we discussed in Chapter 3, it then isn't perceived as impolite and threatening to the face of the various parties. Managing the talk can be accomplished in a number of ways that lead to harmony rather than disharmony between the parties:

- **Managing one's own talk.** Participants can decide what they are going to do with their talk, for example, refusing a request point blank, which would threaten the other speaker's face, or refusing a request by making an alternative offer, which would keep the negotiation alive. For Gulf Arabs with a preference for politeness and indirectness, using less confrontational options rather than a direct rejection would be instrumental in building rapport and maintaining good working relations.
- **Managing the course of the conversation.** Participants can manage the talk by deciding what to talk about and what order to do it in. As we discussed in Chapter 3, high context Gulf Arabs may need much more time on safe, non-negotiation topics than their Western counterparts, before the real negotiation can begin. It can also be a good idea for managers to spend some time talking about the existing professional relationship before moving on into the next business transaction or topic for discussion. Such strategies acknowledge the importance of the relationship.
- **Managing participation.** Speakers can decide how to participate and also how to manage the participation of other speakers in the negotiation. In the Gulf region, this means understanding the power relations between people in the

work context. It may mean, for instance, allowing people to repeat themselves to emphasize or argue a point since this is a feature of communication in the region, as we will discuss in more detail in Chapter 5. Moreover, because of the collectivist nature of many of the national cultures that make up the workforce in the GCC, it may also mean that business people need to give the same information on more than one occasion to different groups of people to make sure that everyone who belongs to the wider group is informed.

- **Choosing a communication style.** Speakers can create harmony in the style of the communication they select. This is reflected in their choice of tone and in the level of formality that they choose to use. Gulf Arabs are typically friendly and have a good sense of humour, as we will discuss in more detail in Chapter 5. However, they are conservative and formal in their dealings with each other and with people from outside their immediate social group. As a result, it is advisable to approach them in a similar way. The same is also the case for people from India and from Pakistan, two of the other major contributors to the workforce in the region.

- **Using appropriate nonverbal communication.** Participants can strengthen or threaten rapport through their use of nonverbal communication, for example, through their posture and gestures and in the way they make eye contact. People from the Gulf, and from the countries that make up much of the workforce, are more aware of their own nonverbal communication and that of others than people from low context Western countries. They are careful about their posture in professional settings, and they do not generally use extravagant gestures. While they do not avoid eye contact entirely, they also use it in a nonthreatening way and do not look constantly at the other speaker. As we have discussed previously, Gulf Arabs are particularly careful in male–female interactions, as professional discussions between the genders are a relatively recent phenomenon in the Gulf workplace.

Managing talk to increase the rapport that exists between the speakers in an interaction is particularly important for speakers from low context cultures. Achieving favorable rapport can create and preserve a work relationship and therefore can have considerable impact on relations with employees from high context cultures. Even a single problematic event that might occur may not be viewed as a failure for a Gulf Arab, as long as the working relationship is still intact.

CHAPTER 5

Negotiation Styles in the Gulf

Arabic argumentation is structured by the notion that it is the pres-entation of an idea [...] that is persuasive, not the logical structure of proof which Westerners see behind the words.[1]

Some studies suggest that the way in which Arabs argue is influenced by the poetic nature of their language; they employ the richness available in Arabic to persuade and convince rather than focusing on logic, as is characteristic of Western cultures.[2] This chapter helps foreign managers develop an awareness of the specific features that are inherent in the argumentation styles used by Gulf Arabs and suggests how managers can participate more effectively in negotiations and discussions that may seem quite different from those they have experienced previously.

Do Gulf Arabs Argue?

We have discussed in Chapter 3 how Gulf nationals are very careful to maintain smooth interactions with others in order to avoid confrontation. This means that they may use argumentation to work toward a business agreement in a different way from their Western counterparts. We will refer to two UAE based studies to serve as an illustration of how Gulf people interact and what motivates their decision to enter into an argument.

One relevant research project was conducted with people from the UAE, the United States, India, and China and attempted to measure their relative levels of argumentativeness and verbal aggressiveness.[3] Verbal aggressiveness refers to the practice of attacking the other person's character and behavior rather than focusing on the topic under discussion. The study found that Emiratis in the sample scored higher than the U.S. nationals and on a par with the Indian and Chinese nationals indicating that the tendency to engage in an argument was stronger than the desire to avoid one among the Emirati, Indian, and Chinese nationals than it was among the U.S. nationals. However, the study also revealed that participants from all four of the nations preferred to maintain good social relationships rather than engage in hostility. Additionally, the Emiratis tended to assign more importance to the impact of the argument on the relationship between the persons involved than did the U.S., Indian, and Chinese subjects. In short, arguing is as important for Emiratis, and perhaps other Gulf people, as it is for other nations in the world. It is not associated with verbal aggressiveness, however, and it is typically conducted in such a way that it does not threaten the relationship with the other party.

Another study comparing UAE and Lebanese nationals showed that the person's character or attitude plays a major role in defining the outcome of argumentative interactions among Emirati nationals who also tend to take conflict more personally than do the Lebanese.[4] This difference can be explained by the importance of trust in personal relationships, which is a cardinal feature of Gulf culture and how relationships are managed.

Cultural Influences on Gulf Negotiation Styles

A high priority is placed on conflict resolution in the Gulf and, indeed, one of the reasons for the creation of the GCC in 1981 was to facilitate the mediation of inter-Arab conflicts in the Middle East.

As discussed in Chapter 3, indirectness is preferred among Gulf nationals but such indirectness does not imply confusion or uncertainty as it might in a low context Western culture. This difference creates a very different approach to negotiation between the high context Gulf Arabs and people from those cultures that practice more direct forms of communication. For example, what may seem to a foreign negotiator to be protracted indecision may simply be the result of indirectness, and the foreigner may be surprised when the negotiation quickly turns into a plan of action. In short, while the indirectness and apparent vagueness in the negotiation reflects the preference of Gulf Arabs to maintain politeness and avoid loss of face for everyone involved, it should not be confused with indecisiveness.

Another cultural issue that comes into play in negotiation situations is the region's high power distance. Fear of not respecting the established hierarchy may lead to hesitation in decision making if the senior person's approval is not clear. Examples of this are frequent in the case of customer service where conflict situations often arise. One study in the UAE concluded that the typical response of Emirati employees experiencing a case of conflict with a customer is that if their boss states that the customer is always right, then the employees will act in accordance with that principle.[5]

As discussed in Chapter 2, the Gulf region is defined as a moderately masculine society meaning that Gulf Arabs may exhibit moderately competitive behavior. The win-lose aspect of oral argumentation and the sense of competition behind it are factors that compel Gulf Arabs to defend their own opinion and be persistent in their objective. However, they would almost never use a competitive negotiation style that is likely to lead to conflict.[6] This behavior contrasts with what is expected in conflict resolution in the Western cultures, where both collaborative and competitive behaviors are seen as positive. Gulf Arabs generally prefer compromise or to avoid conflict entirely.

Tolerance and Compromise

Basic differences in people's opinion, backgrounds, and points of view may cause them to engage in an argument. However, Gulf Arabs are very tolerant of cultural and social diversity and tend to respect the differences between themselves and the expatriates who live in their countries. This is especially evident in their multicultural workplaces where locals are usually in the minority, especially in the private sector. Here the collectivist nature of the Gulf culture comes into play since a high priority is placed on the interests of the group as a whole and on avoiding arguments. Although the local Gulf populations are very different in many ways from the expatriates who make up their workforces, they tend not to focus on their differences in discussion and are known for friendliness and the use of humor in discussions.

Compromise is as a commonly used strategy in conflict resolution, and this dynamic is also evident in negotiation and interpersonal arguing. One study that investigated argumentation in the UAE asked locals about how they feel after an argument.[7] The most common response was that it depends on the outcome: if they win, they feel good; if they lose, they feel bad. This element of challenge and competitiveness also underpins the Gulf Arabs' adoption of a *souq* (Arabic word for market) mentality when bargaining.[8] What this means is that in a bargaining situation the outcome of the transaction depends on the bargaining attitudes of the participants rather than solely on the business outcome. Although bargaining in negotiations can be quite prolonged because of the indirect nature of the arguments used, a final decision usually will be reached. The decision may be unrelated to the argumentation process itself, given that personal relations and practical outcomes are what really matter for Gulf Arabs and not necessarily the process of marshaling the right evidence to support an opinion.

Repetition and Circularity in Discussion

The linguist Barbara Johnstone-Koch claims that Arabic persuasion is based principally on aesthetic and poetic rules, which allow for an idea to be heard again and again until it is remembered.[9] In other words, the presentation and repetition of an idea can be enough to make it believable, and this tendency is rooted in Arabic oral tradition and poetry. Western approaches to argumentation, however, maintain that repetition does not serve any purpose in a discussion and that the reasons given to support a claim should put forward additional information rather than a repetition of the ideas that are already contained in the claim itself. Similarly, counter-arguments should be different from the original claim, while still providing further proof in support of the claim. Arabs, on the contrary, consciously use repetition to express beliefs and viewpoints and a strong emotional attachment to these ideas. They tend to provide supporting arguments that are a repetition of the main argument rather than searching for additional proof to support claims. Such repetition, in combination with an emotional element, will often appear weak and ill-defined to Western counterparts as it contravenes Western norms of nonrepetition and logical rather than emotional appeals.

To summarize, in the context of workplace communication, foreign managers should be aware of the role that repetition can play as a means of expression for Gulf nationals and they should not view this simply as a restatement. The circular and repetitive style of Arab discussion should not be regarded as lacking in method or cohesiveness but rather as an alternative approach to providing a convincing argument.

The Burgeoning Tradition of Debate in the Gulf

Debating practice, shown to be a useful tool for professional training, has been gaining in popularity throughout the Gulf. The rich oral tradition of the region has generated enthusiasm for enhancing public speaking skills. Qatar is developing as a forerunner in debating skills, with its own Debate Centre, which has been part of the Qatar Foundation for Education, Science, and Community Development since 2008. The Centre has also established a Debate Academy that trains individuals from Qatar and beyond in the skill of dialogue, argumentation, and persuasion. The Academy organizes workshops for the trainers of teams of young people who participate in national and international debate competitions. It also organizes the University Arabic Debating Championships in Doha.

The competitions that take place within the Doha Debates follow a particular format that has come to be known as the Qatar Debate Format. They consist of four highly defined speaker roles within each team, strictly enforced time restrictions, as well as the expectation that the speakers will use clearly regulated points of information. After the debate takes place, the audience may ask questions, and then the jury decides on the winning team. Doha Debates has received international recognition and is aired eight times a year on the BBC World News Network.

This growing interest in debate is keenly related to developing leadership communication skills since it helps develop critical thinking, self-regulation, and active learning. As a result, debate training has been welcomed in the GCC countries that focus on leadership skills, especially with regard to women's empowerment. We will return to the issue of leadership communication and women in the next chapter.

CHAPTER 6

Management Styles in the Gulf

If Allah puts anyone in the position of authority over the Muslims'
affairs and he secludes himself (from them), not fulfilling their needs,
wants, and poverty, Allah will keep Himself away from him, not
fulfilling his need, want, and poverty.[1]

Managers new to the region may find the approach to management in the
Gulf quite different from what they have experienced in other parts of the
world. This chapter presents an overview of management styles typical in
the Arab world, and the Gulf in particular. We also consider cultural and
historical reasons behind the management approach commonly used in
the region and identify some cultural issues that may confuse non-Arab
managers. Finally, we discuss the role of women in Gulf management
contexts.

The GLOBE Project and Arab Management Style

The GLOBE (Global Leadership and Organizational Behavior Effectiveness) Project is an ongoing project conducted by an international group
of social scientists and management scholars who study cross-cultural
leadership, the relationship between culture and society, and the effectiveness of organizations and leadership.[2] The current findings of the project
are based on the results of a survey administered to 17,300 middle managers operating in 62 cultures. The study divided participating countries
into culture clusters, and its Middle East cluster included two Gulf countries, namely, Kuwait and Qatar, along with Egypt, Morocco, and Turkey.
The study assessed managerial style in terms of six qualities of culturally
endorsed leadership:

- Charismatic/value-based—focus on high standards, innovation, and decisiveness; attempts to inspire employees by being true to the organization's vision and core values.
- Team-oriented—focus on pride, loyalty, collaboration, and cohesiveness among organizational members; stresses common goals.
- Participative—emphasizes equality, delegates authority, and seeks collaboration in decision making.
- Human-oriented—prioritizes employee welfare, compassion, and generosity; displays patience and support to organizational members.
- Autonomous—an independent, individualistic, and self-centric approach.
- Self-protective—concern with procedure, status-consciousness, and face-saving behaviors; highlights the safety and security of the individual and the group.[3]

The study found that managers within the Middle East cluster scored low on the leadership traits of charisma, participation, and team-orientation, and high in terms of reliance on procedure, face-saving, self-centeredness, status-consciousness, and conflict induction.

Other studies describe Middle Eastern management style in similar terms and illustrate a tendency toward authoritarian and patriarchal styles of leadership.[4] However, more recently a trend toward management by exception (MBE) and a laissez-faire approach has also been identified.[5] MBE refers to a management approach in which employees have autonomy in carrying out their duties and only involve management if exceptional situations arise. Laissez-faire management refers to granting employees considerable freedom in making decisions and conducting their work.

Sociocultural Roots of Gulf Management Style

Naturally, certain cultural traits inherent in the Gulf that we have discussed have influenced the customary approach to management. This includes the high value placed on personal connections and loyalty, people orientation rather than task orientation, a strong open-door policy, a keen sense of duty to stakeholders, a consultative approach to decision making, and prompt conflict management.[6] These management traits reflect the Gulf's robust power distance and hierarchy that we discussed in Chapter 2.

Religious beliefs and the prioritizing of tribal and family values over business demands also have an impact on management practice in the Gulf.[7] The norm of strict compliance with authority, which developed during the Ottoman and European colonial administrations, provides the historical background to the region's acceptance of obedience to authority and centralized decision making. Another factor that plays a significant role in the Gulf approach to management is the attitude to Western influences. Some Gulf nationals perceive Western ideas as modernizing factors while others regard them as corrupting, and such perceptions affect the degree to which individual managers decide to incorporate elements of Western management styles.

In addition, qualities ascribed to the Gulf's early religious leaders, namely, humility, courage, and concern for others, still influence how managers are expected to behave. A consequence of this is that managers who prioritize stability and are conservative and adept at managing personal relationships tend to be well regarded.[8]

Multiple Roles of the Manager and the Concept of "Bedoaucracy"

A significant difference in how the role of manager is conceived in the Arab world as compared to other cultural contexts is the greater number of functions that are considered to be part of the managerial role. Managers in the Arab world are expected *ipso facto* to be better than their subordinates; they are expected to take care of the people who work under them; they are expected to respond to the needs for national development most especially in terms of the workforce localization policies discussed in Chapter 1; and, at the same time, they are expected to promote organizational efficiency as much as possible.

In an attempt to locate these various, sometimes mutually conflicting, demands within a single managerial framework, scholars have developed an alternative management model that is in keeping with Gulf culture.

This has been termed "Bedoaucracy," and it attempts to mesh the managerial role with the traditional Bedouin culture of the region: "It combines elements from both Western models of bureaucracy, with its emphasis on efficiency, and the traditional Bedouin culture with its emphasis on tribal solidarity, collective decision making, and communal welfare."[9]

The expectation that managers will prioritize the care of their employees may seem alien to those from other cultural contexts, most especially when such care is in conflict with organizational goals. Moreover, as discussed in Chapter 3, the importance of relationships can lead to an emphasis on the development of personal associations that might confuse a manager accustomed to a task-focused approach. That is, a manager may feel somewhat disconcerted by overtures of friendship beyond what might seem normal among colleagues or in leader–follower dyads.

Participative Versus Autocratic Management?

In many contexts, both Western and non-Western, a participative, democratic leadership style has been shown to increase employee commitment to the organization.[10] However, this approach may fail if employees expect specific instruction and control from their manager. While many Western managers may feel an inclusive style will lead to enhanced employee engagement and productivity, workers that are accustomed to a more autocratic style may lose respect for a manager who, in seeking to gain their input, may appear to be unsure and unqualified for the managerial role.[11] Arab managers traditionally take an autocratic approach and tend not to delegate authority. Their subordinates typically accept this top-down line of command and have little wish to share power with their managers. Indeed they would generally be wary of their managers' attempts to bring them into the decision-making process.[12]

This tendency toward authoritarian leadership stems from the cultural trait of high power distance discussed in Chapter 2 that is strong among Gulf nationals, as well as among the large numbers of workers from countries such as India, Pakistan, and the Philippines. This high power distance encourages the acceptance of power structures and total obedience to managers. The high uncertainty avoidance that is also a feature of these cultures means that people want things to be clearly defined and regulated. The cultural trait of masculinity, which is also prevalent in these cultures, means that employees expect a certain degree of assertiveness in a manager's identity.[13]

Managers from cultures which display low power distance, low uncertainty avoidance, and very feminine leadership traits will need to think about how best to interact with workers to avoid unnecessarily frustrating employee expectations of managerial behavior.

Birds of a Feather Flock Together: Fragmentation of Workforces

The large numbers of expatriate workers in the Gulf hailing from countries with strongly collectivist cultures are prone to establishing in-groups/out-groups according to nationality. In Chapter 1 we referred to the Similarity Attraction Paradigm, a social-psychological theory that suggests that the more similar people are, the more likely they are to become close to each other and develop alliances.[14] While this "birds of a feather flocking together" dynamic may have positive outcomes in that communication and collaboration among these in-groups can be effective, it can also produce several negative consequences. One issue is that it is more difficult to establish team identity when the team is composed of individuals from different cultures.[15] An additional problem is that in-group loyalty may supersede organizational loyalty, meaning that workers' actions may be motivated more by attempts to support and protect their in-group members than it is by delivering a good performance.

Another serious result of in-group/out-group thinking is that members of an in-group may alienate and ostracize nonmembers, thus making it harder for these individuals to operate within the organization. Those individuals who are perceived as being very different are often excluded from existing alliances within the organization, and it is common for negative stereotype images to be developed about them.[16] As discussed in Chapter 1, this divide is particularly strong in the way in which Gulf workers are viewed by expatriate workers.[17]

Diversity Climate: Embracing and Capitalizing on Difference

The concept of diversity climate has become very important globally, given the increasingly diverse workforces and the need in companies to incorporate all kinds of personal differences within a shared organizational identity. Diversity climate refers to the culture of an organization that not only employs workers who display obvious differences such as gender, age, ethnicity, nationality, and cultural background, but that also establishes mechanisms to celebrate these differences as a potential source of enrichment within the organization and make provision for the different needs of individual workers.[18] It represents a conscious decision and commitment to use value differences as a source of organizational enhancement. In organizations with a positive diversity climate, the tendency for workers to fragment into nationality-based groups is less common and employees can develop a greater sense of company-wide identity, commitment, and task performance.

While creation of a diversity climate is receiving attention in various Western countries such as the United States, it has not been given much importance in the Gulf. As we have discussed, in the Gulf countries, workforce diversity initially came about for extrinsic reasons, that is, the lack of available local workers. It has remained in place partly because of a shortage of local labor but also through an organizational preference for workers whose salary expectations are lower than those of local workers. Against such a background of economically motivated workforce diversity, it is difficult to establish a sense of the equal value of all workers for the organization.

Given the disjointedness of many private sector workforces in the Gulf, there is a need for an overarching culture that can embrace diverse employees within a single identity of organizational goals that benefit both the company and its individual members. Individual managers can contribute to the development of such a diversity climate by focusing on the ways employees interact with each other. That is, managers can establish a code of communication that encourages networking across formal work teams as well as across informal nationality-based groups. Such a code should be in keeping with the local Gulf culture but also accommodate the different communication practices of other cultural groups.[19] In the case of the UAE, for example, local workers have been shown to welcome colleagues from different cultural backgrounds and to appreciate the benefit of their more varied experience. Developing a code of communication relating to personal interactions that capitalizes on this willingness to engage with others could boost the development of a positive diversity culture that would enhance employee relations and lead to greater organizational identity.[20]

Diversity Climate and Trust Within Multinational Workforces

Experienced managers are aware that gaining the trust of employees is crucial in order to secure high morale and good performance. Low levels of trust in management result in limited engagement and contribute to employee turnover. Establishing trust is always a complex issue affected by many variables such as work conditions, job security, and the different personalities of individuals. However, establishing trust can be extremely difficult when the members of the working group are from different cultures and hold different basic assumptions about what is correct behavior as well as very different expectations of the leader-follower relationship.

A bottom-up approach to establishing a diversity climate will work to enhance levels of trust since it will contribute to greater transparency in communication. As discussed in Chapter 3, the role of trust is particularly important given that it is a fundamental element in the operation of the high context cultures that make up the Gulf workforce.

High Context Cultures and the Practice of "Face Time"

The practice of "face time," that is spending long hours in the workplace to make a good impression on bosses and colleagues, needs a special note in the discussion of Gulf workforce practices. The practice of face time in some Western contexts has been shown to demotivate employees who feel they spend too much time in the workplace regardless of the level of productive behavior.[21] However, in more high context cultures, it is part of how individuals expect to behave.

People from high context cultures rely on personal contact to communicate effectively, and they tend to prefer meetings and other face-to-face contact rather than less direct methods including email or phone conversations. This means that managers from Western cultures may find themselves overwhelmed by the need to have meetings about what they consider to be trivial matters that can be handled more efficiently via email or phone. They might also see their subordinates "hanging around" more frequently than they would in other parts of the world.

Micro-Management and High Uncertainty Avoidance Cultures

The notion that keeping track of employees' movements can be counter-productive[22] has not gained popularity in the Gulf. The high uncertainty avoidance that is characteristic of many of the cultures represented in the workforce may lead to levels of micro-management that would not be considered efficient in a Western context.[23] Thus, managers from uncertainty avoiding cultures typically feel compelled to micro-manage their subordinates. Employees from such cultures expect this kind of close supervision and may not respond positively to a less controlling approach. The notion that "When the cat's away, the mice will play" often comes into practice when employees who expect close supervision are assigned to a manager who operates by giving subordinates a greater degree of freedom in their work.

Female Managers in the Gulf

The Gulf is a region where traditional notions of job suitability and gender remain strong;[24] and as observed in Chapter 1, female participation in the workforce remains low. Women are even less visible in management levels, and figures for females serving on company boards of directors in the Middle East have been calculated as being as low as 3.2 percent.[25] Some parts of the Gulf, however, have set greater involvement of women in leadership roles as a national priority; the UAE government in particular has declared its objective of setting "a new benchmark for female empowerment in the region."[26]

Yet, while female involvement in senior business roles is increasing, only 7 percent of the UAE's legislators, senior officials, and managers are female.[27] This limited presence of women in influential roles means that female managers' experiences may be quite different from that of their male counterparts. Research has shown that many Gulf women managers feel they are discriminated against, earn less, and are not respected as much as their male counterparts.[28] However, other research indicates that young Gulf Arabs are shifting away from the traditional patriarchal views on women in managerial roles.[29]

Over recent decades many parts of both the Western and non-Western world have witnessed a shift toward greater gender equality in the workplace and in society in general. However, the Gulf region retains traditional notions of gender and womanhood, and the gender-neutrality that is aspired to within Western organizations (although many claim that it does not actually exist in reality) is not a typical part of the management agenda. In addition to the obstacles faced by women managers in many parts of the world, studies have illustrated that in the Arab world they also have to deal with the challenges posed by the powerful patriarchies of their societies.[30] For instance, in a study of Arab women managers conducted by the Dubai Women Establishment and PricewaterhouseCoopers (PWC), 42 percent of the 96 female Arab leaders interviewed described their countries' legal systems as presenting substantial challenges to women; 44 percent reported the religious environment as unfavorable to women.[31]

Alongside these challenges for female managers in the Gulf, however, there exists a strong element of concern for women that originates in the region's cultural norm of taking care of women and according them special consideration. This concern manifests itself in various ways such as the provision of female-only services in government entities and banks, the existence of a floor for women only in the Abu Dhabi stock exchange, and the general tendency to give women priority in such situations as queues, and so on. This focus on displaying respect for women is also reflected in the managerial context through the tendency of senior organizational members to grant meetings requested by women managers more readily than would be the case if a male manager made a similar request. This privilege allows female managers the opportunity to gain access to higher management and potentially exert greater influence on senior decision making.[32]

Women and Leadership Styles

As discussed earlier in this chapter, a paternalistic—and male—style of leadership is very common in the Gulf.[33] Many organizations in the region continue to operate within this paternalistic, authoritarian style of leadership, particularly those that are family-run businesses. Paternalism does not, however, represent the full picture of management in the Gulf today, and more modern styles of leadership have also become more common in the past few years. The increasing participation of women in leadership means that many organizations no longer exclusively apply traditional styles of leadership. There is evidence that transformational leadership has become much more popular, for instance, particularly among the new wave of female leaders that have risen to prominence.[34] *Transformational leadership* refers to a style of leadership in which managers work collaboratively with their employees and allow them to carry out their tasks autonomously without close control. Very recent work among young educated Gulf Arabs from the UAE, for instance, would suggest that there is a strong preference for collaborative styles of leadership involving autonomy and discussion.[35]

In short, managers from outside the Gulf region need to understand that leadership styles are in a state of flux and that traditional forms of management may coexist alongside more modern ways of managing people.[36] This means that managers need to be sensitive to the expectations of their workforce and develop a management and communication style, or perhaps multiplicity of styles that will resonate most effectively with all its members.

CHAPTER 7

Case Studies

Case Study 1

Localization in the Private Sector

Description: The experience of a local female college graduate who accepts a position in the HR department of a big hotel chain.

Issues to watch for: Localization; minority status of Gulf locals in the private sector workforce; pitfalls of workforce localization implementation; diversity climate; alienation of local workers by expatriate employees; lack of information sharing among expatriate and local employees; employee disengagement.

Sara Al Falasi has recently graduated from a local university with a degree in business with an HR major. She was keen to find a job in the private sector as she felt it would be more exciting than a public sector position. Many of her family members and her friends work in the public sector, and she was aware of the benefits they enjoy such as shorter working hours, days off for all public holidays, many opportunities for further training, and solid promotion prospects. However, being an outgoing and ambitious type, she was drawn to the dynamic culture of the private sector and hoped to develop her career within an MNC or big local company.

Sara applied for and was offered a job in a hotel but decided not to accept the offer, as her parents were not keen on the late hours involved in working in the hospitality sector. She then applied for a position with the same company but working in the HR office in the company's headquarters. She was delighted when she was appointed, and her family was happy since her work schedule involved normal office hours with no late-night shifts.

Sara began her job with great enthusiasm and was thrilled by the number of people from very different countries she got to meet in the company headquarters. She was excited to learn more about her job and was determined to focus all her energies on developing her skills and gaining experience. She dreamed of being a role model for other local women and an inspiration for them to take on demanding roles in the private sector.

In the first week she settled into her new office and attended several meetings. Everyone was very polite and friendly to her. As her job title was that of HR administrator, she expected to be exposed to decision-making activities even if she was just observing, given her lack of experience. She was a little surprised to see the duties assigned to her involved handling employment requests for leave. This was a very straightforward task as she just had to confirm that the employee had adequate leave available and check with the employee's line manager that the dates of the requested leave did not coincide with a very busy period. Another basic task was to check the credentials presented by job applicants to ensure that all of them were correct.

Sara became more baffled when she learned that Annunziata Bruni, her colleague in the department, was invited to attend a meeting on the number and nature of hires for the next six months, but she herself was not. She took the courage to approach her boss, Jonathan Beckett, and ask him why she had not also been invited to attend. Jonathan began his response by saying how very happy he was to have her on his team and commenting on how well she was doing. He told her that he had invited Annunziata as she had been with the company for nine months and had more experience identifying the company's needs. Sara responded politely but she felt confused since being present at a meeting like this would have allowed her to gain a greater understanding of the company's hiring needs.

In the third week of her job she had a visit from another local employee, Khalid Al Suwaidi. She was very happy to meet him since she had not met any other locals in the company so far. She asked him if he had been on leave since she assumed that this was why they had not met before. He told her he hadn't and had been at work every day. He invited her to have coffee in the staff room, and she was happy to join him so that she could learn more about the company. Over coffee she asked him about his work and if he was busy. She was a little surprised by his reply:

"I don't do a lot of work." She asked him to explain and he told her that he had joined the company with a keen interest in making a career within the private sector and that he hoped to develop his potential and handle increasingly difficult tasks. He found, however, that he was assigned little work and the work that he was given was simple and, he felt, beneath his abilities as a bilingual university graduate.

Khalid continued the conversation by explaining that he had been a friend of Majid, another local man, who had left the company recently to take a position in the public sector. Majid had decided that he couldn't stay in the job; while his colleagues were very polite to him, they often failed to tell him about important meetings or share information with him related to his job. If he asked them for advice on how to do something, they would often do the entire thing for him but never explained how it was to be done. Also he was saddened by the fact that his colleagues often had lunch together and even met for dinner on weekends but never invited him to join them. He came to the conclusion that he could never improve his skills in this environment and he resented that. Despite being willing to work and friendly to his colleagues and bosses, he had not developed his professional skills or made friendships within the company.

Khalid went on to talk about other friends he had attended university with who had been recruited to airline companies as part of the workforce localization policies. He said they had felt very welcome within their companies and had been happy with the on-the-job orientation and training they had been given. He also described the impressive career progression of his cousin, Amal, who was very successful in a big MNC operating in the region that she had joined just after graduating.

Sara was a little shocked at the picture that Khalid gave her of the experience that he and Majid had had within the company. She began to see herself as being penalized for being a local amid a large number of expatriate workers. She wondered if she should give in to her frustration with the situation and seek a position elsewhere, or if she should hold on to her dream of being successful in a sector that she now felt seemed to be operating against her. She knew that many locals were very happy in private sector positions, but she began to wonder if these were the exceptions.

Questions for reflection:

1. What can management do to help the locals they recruit integrate into their expatriate-dominated workforce?
2. What communication strategies can be put in place to ensure adequate information exchange between locals and expatriates?
3. How can managers synchronize the behaviors of locals and expatriates in order to build a level playing field for all employees?
4. How can managers develop a positive diversity climate that embraces all employees?

Case Study 2

Business Etiquette in the Gulf

Description: Key intercultural communication issues regarding business etiquette experienced by an expat manager from Canada who had been transferred to Oman.

Issues to watch for: Low versus high time orientation; low versus high context; power distance; saving face; informality versus formality; indirect versus direct communication style.

John Smith, an operations manager at a big multinational oil company, was transferred from the head offices in Calgary to Muscat, the capital of Oman, where the intention was that he would stay for several years in order to manage a regional project. John had 10 years' experience in managing similar projects both in Canada and the United States, but this was his first time living outside of North America. His stay was planned as part of a joint venture in which the Canadian and Omani companies had collaborated for the past two years.

When John arrived at Muscat International airport, he was supposed to meet with the company representatives at the arrivals lounge. Although the time of his flight had been communicated by email long before, he received a phone call to confirm that he was there before the driver appeared at the airport. He was driven to his hotel, where the first meeting with the local project managers was to take place. John was at the hotel lounge ready for the meeting five minutes before the set time. Abdulla and Ahmed, the Omani representatives, arrived half an hour later. The three colleagues spent two hours talking in general about the progress of the joint venture thus far and the projects that were to be completed in the MENA (Middle-East and North Africa) region in the next five years. At several points John asked concrete questions about the way in which projects were usually carried out in Oman and in the wider Gulf Region. Abdulla and Ahmed kindly told him to wait until the formal meeting, which was to be held the next day with all the main company representatives of the other departments.

Although John was fairly tired from his flight and the discussions on the first day, he was informed that a welcome dinner had been organized for him. John thought that this dinner would also involve work, so he took his laptop and some of the main figures and details to share. To his surprise, the dinner was in the desert, at a tourist venue with local entertainment including driving in the sand dunes, riding camels, and smoking shisha. Abdulla and Ahmed arrived a little later in traditional Omani dress, although in the morning they had been wearing suits. While they were eating, John felt ill at ease because of the unexpected informality of the setting. He tried to handle this awkwardness by asking the two men about their families. Both of them said they were married. They didn't mention anything about their wives, but they did talk about their children with a lot of enthusiasm. After a while, Abdulla changed the subject and asked some general things about the customs in North America, typical foods, and traditions. They also explained to John about the Omani traditional dance they were watching.

The meeting the next day started in the late morning. Six other people were present, all project managers from different departments. The local operations manager, Saeed Albannai, arrived late but they all waited for him before beginning the meeting. Saeed introduced John to the other people and he expressed his pleasure and gratitude at having him there. After they had all introduced themselves and talked a little about their various projects, a buffet lunch with typical Arabic food was served in the meeting room. During lunch, Saeed excused himself as he had to leave because of a family issue. John was taken to see his new office, and he also spent some time completing some administrative procedures with the Omani HR department.

During the first two weeks, John found that he was feeling confused about the way in which the Omani company went about its business. He was unsure about how the project groups operated, and he wanted to know what problems his subordinates were facing and what decision-making strategies they used. To make matters worse, he also frequently felt tired; he often had to participate in online meetings with his colleagues at the Calgary headquarters late at night in Oman because of the time difference with North America, or on Fridays—his day off, which meant that he rarely had time to relax.

John decided that he wanted to meet with all of the employees in his department on a more regular basis to gain a better understanding of their work and the main concerns that they were facing. He asked his administrative assistant to call his department together for a meeting using an email invitation. In this email he said that the meeting would be about the distribution of tasks and some possible changes to the company's operations procedures in the region. He thought that it would be a good idea to invite everyone in the department so that they could all voice their opinions. To his surprise, only Ahmed and Abdulla appeared at the scheduled time for the meeting, which turned into a general friendly discussion about the objectives for the year, without any concrete decisions being made.

After about a month, John felt that he had started to figure out how things worked in the Omani company. However, he still had difficulties in meeting with his subordinates as they preferred to communicate through their local managers. John was worried that he would never be able to manage the operations of the company effectively. In addition, in a private communication, Saeed told John that many employees had complained that he was overly direct and interfering. He mentioned, for instance, that John's frequent emails outlining procedures to follow were viewed as overbearing as the employees were not used to this type of communication. They were accustomed to informal lunch meetings during which their direct managers communicated what was to be done and how. Emails were only sent to follow up on these meetings, or in urgent situations to outline concrete tasks that needed to be completed.

After this insightful discussion with Saeed, John understood better how to adapt to the local communication needs and attitudes. With continuous advice from Ahmed and Abdulla, who were always willing to help, John began to talk and write in ways that were more acceptable to his subordinates. He opted for several informal meetings instead of writing long emails, and he also took the initiative to visit people's offices to say hello or to have tea with them. This was very much appreciated; people started trusting John more and they showed a greater willingness to collaborate in implementing the changes he proposed.

Questions for reflection:

1. What are the main business communication style differences between John and the Omanis?
2. What do you think was the major concern of the Omanis when John took on his new role? What did they do to help John adapt?
3. Why did John feel frustrated at the beginning of his stay in Oman?
4. What would you recommend to other managers coming to the Gulf from low context countries such as Canada, the United States, or the United Kingdom? What should they do to adapt their style of communicating and conducting business to be more effective in the Gulf context?

Case Study 3

The Use of Business English in the Gulf

Description: The challenges faced by an English-speaking manager who is sent to Kuwait City to manage one of the engineering departments for an international corporation providing support services for the oil industry.

Issues to watch for: Accommodation; the variety of languages spoken in the Gulf; the need to take into account different communication styles in English; horizontal communication; the effects of corporate language policy.

Pete Stevens is a senior manager from the United Kingdom who has recently been transferred from his company's Houston office in the United States to manage a group of around 200 engineers based in the regional office in Kuwait City. Although this group consists of many of the company's best engineers and has the reputation for dealing effectively with complex, and often difficult projects, it has also experienced high levels of attrition in the 12 months prior to Pete's transfer. Indeed, several of the top engineers have recently left to join a competitor. Pete has worked for the company for 15 years, starting in London, as a junior engineer, and working his way up through the ranks until his last five-year position in the United States. Although he has visited the Gulf region on numerous occasions earlier in his career to work on different engineering projects, this is his first time managing in a country where English is not the dominate language.

On the morning of his first day at work, his department gathered in the main auditorium for him to meet everyone. Pete was interested to see that his staff included a group of what looked to him like local women, in a combination of national and Western dress, and a larger group of Omani men, wearing their distinctive turbans or colorfully embroidered caps. Apart from this, there were a large number of Indian men, and a much smaller number of men and women who could have been from Eastern or Western Europe, or perhaps from Lebanon. Within the group of people wearing Western style business dress, there was also a number of people from the United States who Pete already knew were engineers who were often sent over from Houston to Kuwait City for a short period of time to increase their understanding of the company. All of his employees appeared to be sitting with either their own or a closely related national group.

As Pete entered the room he noticed that many languages other than English were being spoken and he recognized the sound of Arabic, Hindi, Russian, and Italian. Pete introduced himself to his department and talked a little about his plans for the future and then opened the floor for questions and discussion. Many of the Indian engineers asked questions, as did almost all the employees from Europe and several other people who he recognized from the Houston office. None of the Omani men or Kuwaiti women participated, although Pete noted that they were paying close attention to what was being said. Once the session was over, Pete wondered why the Gulf nationals in the room had been much more reluctant to contribute than the other nationalities. He asked Paolo Rizzato, one of his direct reports from Italy, why he thought this had happened and Paolo laughed and said they were always like that.

In the weeks that followed, Pete had many opportunities to meet with smaller groups of his employees, sometimes in formal meetings and sometimes in informal discussions. He found that the Indian, Italian, and Lebanese employees often spoke so quickly that he was unable to catch what they were saying, and they constantly interrupted each other and other people. The Gulf employees, on the other hand, rarely took a turn unless it was offered to them explicitly by the chair in a meeting, and they took much more time in formulating what they had to say. The Gulf women in particular had difficulty in entering a discussion and were very likely to allow other speakers to take the floor from them if they were interrupted or challenged. Despite this apparent reluctance to engage, Pete noted that they invariably made excellent and technically sound suggestions. Pete realized that he needed to take action to make sure all of his employees' voices were heard and that everyone felt comfortable enough to participate in meetings and discussions.

Pete put a taskforce together of employees representing all the different nationalities within his department, and he asked them to talk to everyone and find out how they thought the communication across the department could be improved. He asked them to identify who they usually talked to and why, and what they thought were the challenges that stopped them from talking to other people. When they reported back to him the following week, his staff had a number of interesting things to say.

First of all, just about everyone agreed that their English language skills were good enough to cope with the demands of the job, both in speaking and in writing. Almost everyone had completed their university education in English, and many had attended an English-medium high school in their home country. A few people mentioned that they would like to improve their writing skills in English, but that they were comfortable speaking English. Several people mentioned the fact that they had problems getting used to all the different accents in the department, especially given the speed at which both the Indian and British employees spoke. Many of the Omani and Kuwaiti employees commented on the fact that they were much more familiar with American English, and that they sometimes found it difficult to understand the words that their Indian colleagues used. Many people mentioned that they struggled in general with the native English speakers in the department, particularly when they were talking about something together; they talked too fast and used lots of expressions that no one else could understand. Many of the employees commented that they were annoyed when other nationalities used languages other than English to discuss things amongst themselves, although other people said that it often helped them to be able to clarify a difficult point in their own first language and then switch back into English. Given this they often gravitated toward their own nationality and tried to work with them.

Second, people talked about the different styles of communicating that other people used that they often found difficult to deal with. As Pete had already observed, many employees complained about the fact that the Indians and Italians interrupted everyone all the time, held several conversations at once, and spoke very fast. The Gulf Arabs and North Americans in particular found this offensive, and they couldn't understand why they needed to speak so quickly and to use many words to say what they wanted to say. On the other hand, the Indians especially found that the Gulf Arabs were too introverted and indirect, and often very slow to respond, and they expressed frustration that the Kuwaiti women in particular hardly ever participated in large group discussions, although they knew that they had something valuable to contribute.

When he heard what his employees had to say, Peter knew that some of his employees needed training to improve their communication skills. He also knew that, if he was going to keep the levels of attrition in his department from increasing further, he needed to put a new communication plan in place.

Questions for reflection:

1. What can management do to accommodate the different communication styles that exist in the workforce?
2. What can management do to make sure that everyone contributes to discussions in the workplace?
3. What kind of communication training should managers provide for new employees when they enter the workforce in the Gulf region?
4. What should native speakers of English in particular pay attention to when they are working in a multicultural situation?

Case Study 4

Negotiation Styles in the Gulf

Description: In view of the recent introduction of the Wage Protection System (WPS) in Qatar (www.ey.com/GL/en/Services/Tax/Human-Capital/HC-Alert--Qatar-Government-introduces-new-wage-protection-system-requiring-salaries-to-be-paid-into-Qatar-based-accounts), the HR department of a big construction company in Doha needs to decide which cash flow management system to implement.

Issues to watch for: Different negotiation styles; motivation for argumentation; conflict management.

The HR management team of a large, locally-owned construction company in Qatar consists of four members: the HR Director Hamad AlHammadi, a Qatari, and three HR Executives, Keith Bernard, a Canadian, Sarah Badran, a Lebanese, and Kavya Chaudhri, an Indian. After a recent change in the law in Qatar that mandates every organization to implement a unified payroll system controlled by the Central Bank, the HR team needs to make an urgent decision on which product to buy in order to comply with the new cash flow processes since the existing system does not meet the new legal requirements.

The company, based in Doha, has been in operation for 25 years and employs around 15,000 workers from all over the world, the majority being semiskilled Indian and Bangladeshi construction workers. The recently introduced WPS is a government initiative aimed at protecting all employees in Qatar by guaranteeing that their salaries are paid regularly and correctly. The HR team has identified two innovative cash flow management electronic tools that could address the new requirements. The first tool was designed by a local bank and has been shown to meet all the legal requirements. The second is an internationally known HR platform that has been used with great success in the MENA region for the last five years. The company already employs this platform for several other HR-related tasks. The team needs to arrange a meeting to make an immediate decision as to which system to purchase.

All four members of the HR management team have considerable experience in decision making. Keith is the most experienced in various

HR management positions. Kavya has recently been nominated as the best employee of the month in the HR department due to her superb communication skills and the excellent reviews she received from many of the employees. Hammed and Sarah are the only Arabic speakers in the team. Hammed was appointed as director three years ago, and upper management seems to be very satisfied with his performance. Sarah moved with her family from Lebanon to Qatar almost 20 years ago and worked for 10 years in various other companies before joining the firm.

During the meeting, the team learns that they fall into two opposing sides. Hamad and Kavya favor the tool designed by the local bank. Keith and Sarah have a strong preference for the second tool due to its international success and the company's existing familiarity with it. Hamad opens the meeting explaining the pros and cons of each of the tools. He then elaborates on the excellent performance of the first and its reliability, stressing the fact that it originated in a local bank. Kavya expresses her strong agreement with Hamad, also pointing out that, as the central wage payment will be controlled by the Central Bank, it is obvious that having a cash flow management system designed by another local bank is a guarantee of absolute compatibility.

Keith does not express his disagreement directly. Instead, he focuses on the disadvantages of both platforms, most especially from the technical point of view. After his overview in which he gives several concrete examples, he concludes that it would be wiser to opt for the international system since it would present fewer technical risks than the locally designed system. Sarah agrees with Keith and adds that whatever they decide they should be careful about the consequences of implementing something that might only remain up-to-date for the short term. She says that although the first tool was launched as a perfect match for the new wage policy, the additional functions provided by the second tool mean that it also complies with the company's legal requirements for handling visas and expatriate benefits. She feels that they should go for an expanded version of the second tool, with the proviso that they can always change at some point in the future if it fails to meet their needs. Keith adds that just because the first tool was locally designed, that doesn't mean that it will meet their needs best.

Hamad says that he thinks that they are all right and that he wouldn't mind opting for the second tool, apart from the fact that he is being put under pressure from his superiors to choose the first one. He explains that the founder of the bank that had introduced the first tool is an eminent person in the Doha community, and it would be viewed very positively if their company established some form of collaboration with the bank. He also said that he doesn't trust the second tool as it was developed by a company with no knowledge of Qatari standards on salary payments, and they did not collaborate with any other Qatari company in relation to compliance with the new law. Moreover, the international provider's experience in the MENA region is too short to understand how local companies operate. Sarah replies to Hamad saying that as a company, they need to look forward and not simply repeat what other local companies are doing. Having the combination of a local operation with international quality standards would be more innovative than opting for a local partnership. Hamad replies that she is probably right but that it is not their job to provide innovation; their task is to decide on a reliable and efficient HR cash flow management system. Kavya agrees with Hamad.

After a short silence, Keith says they have to move forward with the decision. If they voted it is clear that the result would be split. Therefore, he suggests that each person give his or her strongest argument in favor of and against each tool. They could then make a more considered decision. Hamad, however, kindly asks them to postpone taking a decision. He says that the situation is more complicated than it appears, and important long-term negotiations could potentially be at risk. He suggests that they arrange another meeting the following week. Before that, he plans to get concrete advice and guidelines from his superiors as to what should be done. He thanks his colleagues for their valuable contributions and asks Kavya who was taking notes to circulate the minutes of the meeting.

Questions for reflection:

1. Do you think that the team members' negotiation behavior was due to cultural differences? If yes, what were the major differences among them?

2. Why do you think Hamad suggested postponing the decision? How did he manage this with his colleagues?

3. How would you characterize the conflict management behavior of each one of the team participants?

4. What type of argumentation style did each of the participants use?

Case Study 5

Diversity Climate in the Gulf Region

Description: The challenges faced by a manager from the United States who takes on a position in Abu Dhabi in the UAE as the senior vice president for marketing for one of the national oil companies in the Emirate.

Issues to watch for: Diversity; the understanding of diversity and diversity climate in the Gulf; the need to facilitate communication between different groups; horizontal communication; the effects of local Gulf culture.

Pat Jones is a marketing manager from the United States who has been working for more than 25 years in different corporations and in different parts of the States. He has just arrived in Abu Dhabi to take up a position as Vice President for Marketing for one of the national oil corporations operating in the Emirate. Pat is used to managing large groups of people—his last department at a U.S. oil corporation in New Orleans had more than 200 employees—and he has always actively encouraged his staff to take advantage of any of training opportunities that the corporation offered to them. He has frequently coordinated with the HR department in corporations he has worked for to arrange for his employees to follow internal training courses, including the extensive courses in diversity training that many major U.S. corporations offer.

Pat has also taken numerous diversity-training courses himself and done his best to keep himself up-to-date on the current developments in the field. He therefore feels that he has a reasonably good understanding of how to create a positive diversity climate for all the people working for him. He has visited the Gulf only once before to be interviewed for his new job, and apart from a short stint in Calgary, Canada, he has not worked outside of the continental United States.

When Pat arrives in Abu Dhabi, he spends the first few weeks getting to know his employees. As Vice President for Marketing, he is responsible for a department of around 150 employees, all of who are working at the corporation's head office just off the Corniche in the center of the city. About 40 of his employees are Emirati nationals, in positions at several different levels in his department, and the rest of the staff are mostly from India, with a very small number of Syrians and Filipinos. Almost all his employees, both males and females, are young, most of them under 35.

Incoming projects are typically assigned to teams in consultation with him, with one team leader in charge of four or five employees. Depending on the nature of the project, these teams are usually made up of different ranks and different nationalities. Pat notices early on that his employees are friendly toward each other, and English is used almost all of the time. However, the different nationality groups usually opt to share offices and always sit together at lunch. He notices in particular that while the women appear happy to work together with their male colleagues on projects within the department, they generally do not socialize with them or sit with them at lunch, and they never attend events outside of working hours. Pat is concerned that the women are being marginalized within his department and that his employees are not really capitalizing on the many advantages that multicultural, diverse, teams can bring to an organization.

Pat remembers a course he attended while working for an oil corporation in New Orleans that was specifically designed to encourage teamwork between all of the diverse groups that made up the workforce at the corporation. It included workshops with numerous awareness-raising exercises on a number of different themes such as gender, race, sexuality, ethnic groups, and religion. Pat had found this both challenging and useful, and he knew that it had promoted a lot of discussion at the corporation in Louisiana and had also led to an improvement in both teamwork and productivity. He felt that something like this would benefit his employees in Abu Dhabi. He went to see the head of HR, Kate Nesbitt, who is originally from the United Kingdom, to find out whether the company offered similar courses.

Kate explained that many of the things that are routinely discussed in diversity training courses in the United States are not appropriate for the Gulf context for different reasons. Different religions are tolerated in the UAE for instance, and people are free to practice as they wish, but everyone accepts that the State religion is Islam. In addition, people don't talk openly about social issues such as same sex marriage, as they might do on a diversity-training course in Western contexts, because same sex relationships (and relationships outside of marriage) are not allowed under Sharia law and are therefore not open to debate. Other issues such as race, gender, and ethnicity would also have a very different meaning for people from the Gulf, as well as for many of the people from outside the Gulf who work there. Some non-Western societies may be much more conservative in terms of women's empowerment, for instance, and they may define a person on a very different set of parameters than would normally be the case in the West, including whether or not a person is a member of a prominent family, or of a particular tribal group or community.

After his conversation with Kate, Pat understands that if he is to encourage his employees to collaborate more with each other, he will not be able to rely on Western models of how to develop a positive diversity climate. Pat puts a taskforce together, made up of Fatma Al Qasimi and Mohammad Alhammadi from the UAE, Srinivasan Rao and Sameena Khan from India, Rosita Baxel from the Philippines, and Ahmed Kamel from Syria. He tells them that they need to talk to their colleagues to find ways of creating a positive and inclusive atmosphere within the department so that everyone feels willing to participate and share their ideas.

After a week or two they come back to him with the following ideas for discussion. Fatma and Mohammad talk about the fact that all of the Emirati employees have told them that they are very happy to work alongside their expatriate colleagues and that they feel they have a great deal to learn from them. They both say that their colleagues have told them that they would like more formal ways of interacting with the different people in the department, and not just when they are assigned to the same project together. Srinivasan and Sameena talk about the huge diversity within the Indian employees in the group and the fact that the (predominantly Western) management at the company does not really take this into consideration. As Muslim women, both Fatma and Sameena explain that they do not feel comfortable in mixed company at after-work social occasions and that they therefore prefer not to attend even though they know that these would be useful opportunities to network. Finally, Rosita and Ahmed both complain that they, and their other Filipino and Syrian colleagues, often feel overwhelmed by the large numbers of Emirati and Indian employees, and that they feel their opinions are not always properly taken into account.

Pat listens to the discussion. It's clear that all of his employees are committed to the department's future, and they want to find ways together of making sure it is successful. He knows that he needs to create more formal networking opportunities that will include everyone and take the needs of the different cultural groups into account. He has observed that there are a number of different informal networks within his department that could also be a part of that process. He also realizes that the local employees are an important group that can help him in this task because their willingness to engage with and learn from others could help to create a specific type of organizational culture based on the shared creation of new ideas.

While this process is very different from the way in which he was trained to create a positive diversity climate in the other organizational contexts in which he worked, he can see that this may be successful in the Gulf. Finally, he understands from the discussions with his taskforce that some of his minority employees feel that their opinions are not taken sufficiently into account, and he resolves to find ways of allowing their voices to be heard more often and in a formal way. He concludes from what he has heard that the most important thing for many of the nationality groups working for him is that their colleagues trust them and have confidence in their professional abilities. He sits down with his taskforce and starts to draft a new communication plan for the future.

Questions for reflection:

1. How do the concepts of diversity and diversity climate differ in Western contexts when compared to the Gulf region?
2. What can management do to create a positive diversity climate in a multicultural workplace setting in the Gulf?
3. How can management ensure that everyone's opinion is heard?
4. What role could the local workforce play in the creation of a positive diversity climate?

Case Study 6

Culturally Dissonant Management Styles

Description: Local workers, local styles: The experience of a local bank employee.

Issues to watch for: Culturally diverse teams; participative leadership; autocratic management; micro-management; employee welfare; communication patterns; duty of care.

Mohamed Al Sudairi, a Gulf national, has been working in a privately owned bank for two years, having graduated from a UK university with a degree in Finance. Until three months ago his immediate supervisor was Xavier Alexander, a man from the United Kingdom with a degree in banking. Xavier was then promoted to the position of branch manager. A new recruit, Ganesh Bose, an Indian with a postgraduate business degree from the Indian Institute of Management Bangalore, was appointed as Mohamed's immediate supervisor.

While Xavier was his supervisor, Mohamed was used to taking a lot of initiative and only consulted Xavier when unusual or very sensitive issues arose. Xavier practiced a participative approach and always welcomed Mohamed's suggestions regarding work and customer-related banking practices. Mohamed felt he had a lot of freedom which he accepted with a strong sense of responsibility to the bank and its customers. When Xavier was absent from the bank due to outside meetings or leave, he informally deputized Mohamed to take decisions on all urgent matters. Mohamed had Xavier's mobile phone number in case he needed to consult with Xavier before taking any decisions. However, in almost two years of working Xavier's supervision and being left in charge, Mohamed had never needed to call him. He was careful to follow bank protocol and was skillful in deferring important decisions until Xavier's return.

Mohamed's work pattern changed dramatically after Ganesh became his supervisor. On his first day, Ganesh called Mohamed into his office and told him that strict punctuality was insisted on by the bank. He stressed that bank protocol should be followed without deviation. Anything that could not be covered by this protocol was to be referred to him immediately. He also talked at length about issues such as eating and drinking at one's work desk and visiting the washroom or the prayer room. This "meeting" lasted more than 20 minutes during which time Mohamed had no opportunity to say anything. Ganesh closed the interaction by saying Mohamed should return to his duties.

Mohamed left Ganesh's office feeling confused and somewhat offended. Ganesh's insistence on punctuality was completely unnecessary since Mohamed always arrived at the office 10 or 15 minutes before his official work time began. He did go to the prayer room regularly but spent no more than five minutes there on each occasion. He often ate lunch at his desk but this was mainly because he didn't want to spend too much time away from his work. However, he felt confident that his excellent record with the bank was enough for him to have no concern about the new regime being introduced in his department.

After one month Mohamed received an internal phone call from Salwa Al Mutairi, a student who worked with the bank on Saturdays. She was in her second year at university and was married with a one-year-old daughter. Salwa was very upset and said that Ganesh had called her into his office to warn her about her late arrival on three of the previous four Saturdays. On the first two days she had arrived only five minutes late. This slight lateness had never been commented on before since she was a good worker and was efficient in her duties. On the third Saturday she had arrived half an hour late, as she had first needed to drive to the pharmacy for some medicine as her baby had a slight fever. She had phoned her colleague, Sugita, to ask her to explain her situation to Ganesh and Sugita had done this. The following week Salwa came to the bank to tender her resignation. She told Sugita and Mohamed that, while she had always looked forward to her Saturday work in the bank, it had now become stressful and unpleasant for her. Sugita tried to convince her to stay. She argued that Ganesh was a little strict because he was anxious to make sure that things ran smoothly in the bank. Salwa replied that everyone in the bank was keen to make sure that they did all their work well and that it was unnecessary to pester people about things they were already doing and to scold them for the slightest deviation. She added that every employee was a person with a family and life outside the bank so it was to be expected if a personal issue caused an employee to be late or absent once in a while.

One Thursday afternoon, Ganesh called Mohamed to his office to ask why he had not provided the full documentation for a customer loan. Mohamed explained that the customer's passport was being renewed, so he had provided a copy of his expired passport. Ganesh said that no loan application could be considered in the absence of any required document. Mohamed said that he knew this but that the customer in question had been with their branch for eight years, held substantial investments with the bank, and needed a short-term loan to buy a used car with cash. Ganesh argued that this was a deviation from required practice and that the customer's application could not be considered until he had a new passport. Mohamed went to look for Xavier to ask his opinion. Xavier agreed that since the customer was long-standing and reliable, the application could be processed since the bank could expect to receive the updated passport copy within a week or two. He phoned Ganesh to tell him to process the application, and Ganesh handled the matter without saying anything.

The following week it became clear to Mohamed that Ganesh was very unhappy about what had happened. He began to check Mohamed's behavior and query him when he left his desk to go anywhere. He often followed him into the staff coffee room and waited while Mohamed prepared a coffee to take back to his desk. Although Mohamed viewed this as silly and trivial, he was not disturbed by it.

Two months later Xavier invited Mohamed to his office. He told him that he had put Mohamed's name forward for promotion to section supervisor as Ganesh was leaving their bank; headquarters had endorsed this promotion. Mohamed was delighted and took up his position with great enthusiasm deciding to practice the kind of supervision that he had experienced with Xavier.

In his new role Mohamed consulted with staff members, considered their feedback carefully, held brief, regular meetings in the attempt to gather input on how customer relations could be enhanced. He was given permission to run a pilot project on flexible working hours so that employees could alter their arrival and departure times by up to one hour. His subordinates were delighted with this as it meant they would have more control over how they managed their personal responsibilities during the working day. He was charged by Xavier to develop a detailed report on the impact of this flexi-time project on banking operations since the bank would consider implementing this nationwide if the results were positive in their branch. Mohamed was happy to invest much time and thought into this project as he looked forward to developing a practice that would enhance employee welfare and productivity within the bank.

Questions for reflection:

1. What cultural patterns underlie the different approaches adopted by Xavier and Ganesh in the same role?
2. Why did the local employees react negatively to Ganesh's style of management?
3. What did Xavier do in his supervisory role that enhanced working relations and hence morale and productivity?
4. How can we account for the style of communication adopted by Ganesh?
5. What cultural patterns would encourage Xavier to give his employees a certain amount of control in conducting their duties?
6. Suggest some ways in which a manager of a multicultural team can respond to the diverse ideas about management style held by employees with different nationalities?

Notes

Introduction

1. http://www.forbesmiddleeast.com/en/lists/read/1970/top-500-companies-in-the-arab-world-2014/listid/177/page/1/
2. Hertog (2012).
3. Munif (2002).
4. http://gulfmigration.eu/total-population-and-percentage-of-nationals-and-non-nationals-in-gcc-countries-latest-national-statistics-2010-2015/
5. Al-Ebraheem (1996).
6. Herb (2009).
7. Mehlum and Ostensad (2011).
8. Hofstede (2011).
9. Hall (1976).

Chapter 1

1. Mehlum and Ostensad (2011, p. 1).
2. Mehlum and Ostensad (2011).
3. Swailes, Al Said, and Al Fahdi (2012).
4. Swailes et al. (2012).
5. Forstenlechner and Rutledge (2011).
6. Bahrain Census (2010).
7. Tamkeen (2006).
8. Millington (2009).
9. Hertog (2014).
10. Al Hasan (2012).
11. Maddy-Weitzman (1997).
12. Looney (1992).
13. Nagy Eltony (2007).
14. Al-Mutairi, Naser, and Fayez (2014).

15. Hertog (2014).

16. Swailes et al. (2012).

17. Al-Lamki (1998).

18. Haque (2014).

19. Rejimon (2014).

20. *Doha News* (2013).

21. Hertog (2014).

22. Walker (2014).

23. Hertog (2014).

24. Mustafa (2013).

25. Fatany (2014).

26. Cordesman (2003).

27. Fatany (2014).

28. Schwab (2015).

29. Salem and Dajani (2013).

30. Trenwith (2013).

31. *Doha News* (2011).

32. WEF (2014).

33. Al Qasimi (2007, p. 34).

34. Al Gergawi (2008), Al-Waqfi and Forstenlechner (2012),
    Forstenlechner and Rutledge (2011).

35. Hertog (2013).

36. Bell (2014).

37. Salem (2010).

38. Rejimon (2014).

39. Mustafa (2013).

40. Marois (2012).

41. Al-Waqfi and Forstenlechner (2012).

42. Byrne (1971).

43. Al-Waqfi and Forstenlechner (2012).

Chapter 2

1. Hofstede (1980, pp. 21–23).

2. www.grovewell.com/pub-GLOBE-intro.html

3. www.geert-hofstede.com

4. Hofstede (2011, p. 9).

5. Hofstede (2011, p. 11).

6. Hofstede (2011, p. 10).

7. Hofstede (2011, p. 12).

8. Hofstede (2011, p. 13).

9. Hofstede (2011, p. 15).

10. Salzman (2008).

11. Knight, Mitchell, and Gao (2009).

12. Weiss (1998).

13. Schwab (2015).

14. Hofstede (2011, p. 10).

15. According to www.geert-hofstede.com, this is a speculative score and is not based on empirical data.

16. Hall (1976).

17. McGinley (2012).

18. Goby and Nickerson (2015a).

19. Feghali (1997).

20. Cunningham and Sarayrah (1993).

21. www.waywordradio.org/wasta_1/

22. Al-Ali (2008).

23. Harry (2007).

24. Hawley (2000).

Chapter 3

1. Hall (1976, p. 91).

2. Hall (1976).

3. Locker and Kaczmarek (2013).

4. Trompenaars (1994, p. 89).

5. Planken (2005).

6. Holland (2013).

7. Zaharna (1995, p. 245).

8. Zaharna (1995, p. 250).

9. Johnstone-Koch (1983).

10. Johnstone-Koch (1990).

11. Poyatos (1983).

12. Kaplan (2011).

13. Aslani, Ramirez-Marin, Semnani-Azad, Brett, and Tinsley (2013).

14. Feghali (1997).

15. Hall (1966).

16. Goffman (1955, p. 213).

17. Zane and Yeh (2002).

18. Chan, Wan, and Sin (2009, p. 292).

19. Haase (2013).

20. Loosemore and Muslmani (1999, p. 97).

21. Hofstede (2011, p. 8).

22. Haase (2014).

23. Halligan (2006).

24. Hall (1966).

Chapter 4

1. Louhiala-Salminen, Charles, and Kankaanranta (2005, p. 404).

2. Randall and Samimi (2010).

3. Randall and Samimi (2010).

4. Louhiala-Salminen et al. (2005).

5. Turner and West (2010).

6. Louhiala-Salminen et al. (2005).

7. Rogerson-Revell (2010).

8. Spencer-Oatey (2000).

Chapter 5

1. Johnstone-Koch (1983, p. 55).

2. Hatim (1990); Johnstone-Koch (1983, 1987).

3. Rapanta and Hample (2015).

4. Rapanta and Badran (2015).

5. Jones (2007).

6. Jones (2007).

7. Rapanta and Badran (2015).

8. Jones (2007).

9. Johnstone-Koch (1983, 1987).

Chapter 6

1. Hadith no. 2942 quoted from Beekun (2012).
2. House, Hanges, Javidan, Dorfman, and Gupta (2004).
3. www.inspireimagineinnovate.com/pdf/globesummary-by-michael-h-hoppe.pdf
4. Kassem and Habib (1989).
5. Yaseen (2010).
6. Scott-Jackson (2010).
7. Scott-Jackson (2010).
8. Cunningham and Sarayrah (1993).
9. Kassem and Habib (1989, p. 17).
10. Wu, Tsai, Fey, and Wu (2006); Zeffane (1995).
11. Kassem and Habib (1989).
12. Kassem and Habib (1989).
13. Kabasakal and Bodur (2002).
14. Byrne (1971).
15. Earley and Mosakowski (2000).
16. Tsui and O'Reilly (1989).
17. Goby (2015).
18. Goby, Nickerson, and David (2015).
19. Goby and Nickerson (2015b).
20. Goby et al. (2015).
21. Munck (2001); Simpson (1998).
22. Gurnett (2012).
23. Merchant (2011).
24. Ameen (2001).
25. Natividad (2010).
26. *Women in the United Arab Emirates: A portrait of progress* (2009).
27. Abdalla (2015).
28. Tlaiss (2013).
29. Mostafa (2004).
30. Jamali, Sidani, and Safieddine (2005).
31. DWE (2009).
32. Alhadhrami (2013).
33. Kasseem and Habib (1989).

34. DWE (2009); Abdalla and Al-Homoud (2001).

35. Nickerson and Goby (2016).

36. Smith, Achoui, and Harb (2007).

References

Abdalla, I. A. (2015). Being and becoming a leader: Arabian Gulf women managers' perspectives. *International Journal of Business and Management, 10*(1), 25–39. doi:10.5539/ijbm.v10n1p25

Abdalla, I. A., & Al-Homoud, M. A. (2001). Exploring the implicit leadership theory in the Arabian Gulf states. *Applied Psychology: An International Review, 50*(4), 506–531. doi:10.1111/1464-0597.00071

Al Gergawi, M. (2008, September 11). Emiratisation and the curse of entitlement. *The National*. Retrieved from www.zawya.com/blogs/mishaal/080912081800/

Al Hasan, H. T. (2012, July 8). Bahrain bids its economic reform farewell. openDemocracy. Retrieved from www.opendemocracy.net/hasan-tariq-al-hasan/bahrain-bids-its-economic-reform-farewell

Al Qasimi, L. B. K. (2007). Women in the mainstream. In T. A. Kamali (Ed.), *An anthology celebrating the twentieth anniversary of the Higher Colleges of Technology* (pp. 33–35). Abu Dhabi, UAE: The HCT Press.

Al-Ali, J. (2008). Emiratisation: Drawing UAE nationals into their surging economy. *International Journal of Sociology and Social Policy, 28*(9/10), pp. 365–379. doi:10.1108/01443330810900202

Al-Ebraheem, Y. H. (1996). Kuwait's economic travails. *Middle East Quarterly, 3*(3), pp. 17–23.

Al-Lamki, S. M. (1998). Barriers to Omanization in the private sector: The perceptions of Omani graduates. *The International Journal of Human Resource Management, 9*(2), 377–400. doi:10.1080/095851998341143

Al-Mutairi, A., Naser, K., & Fayez, F. (2014). Employees and managers attitude towards privatization programs: Evidence from an emerging economy. *International Journal of Economics and Finance, 6*(12), 95–109. doi:10.5539/ijef.v6n12p95

Al-Waqfi, M., & Forstenlechner, I. (2012). Of private sector fear and prejudice: The case of young citizens in an oil-rich Arabian Gulf economy. *Personnel Review, 41*(5), 609–629. doi:10.1108/00483481211249139

Alhadhrami, A. (2013). UAE work environment: Examining the influences of culture, gender, and sector on managerial leadership competencies, job satisfaction and organizational commitment (PhD dissertation, Curtin University, Australia). Retrieved from http://espace.library.curtin.edu.au/cgi-bin/espace.pdf?file=/2014/07/28/file_1/199889

Ameen, I. (2001) *Women: Identity difficulties and challenging future.* Beirut, Lebanon: Daralhadi Publication.

Aslani, S., Ramirez-Marin, J., Semnani-Azad, Z., Brett, J. M., & Tinsley, C. (2013). Dignity, face, and honor cultures: Implications for negotiation and conflict management. In M. Olekalns & W. L. Adair (Eds.), *Handbook of research on negotiation* (pp. 249–282). Cheltenham, UK: Edward Elgar Publishing Ltd.

Bahrain Census (2010). Census summary result 2010. Retrieved from www.cio. gov.bh/CIO_ARA/English/Publications/Census/2011%2009%2018%20 Final%20English%20Census%202010%20Summary%20%20Results%20 -%20Review%201.pdf

Beekun, R. (2012, September 9). Leadership and Islam. Retrieved from http:// theislamicworkplace.com/leadership-and-islam/

Bell, J. (2014, February 3). Young generation of Emiratis wants a career not just a job, summit told. *The National.* Retrieved from www.thenational.ae/uae/ emiratisation/young-generation-of-emiratis-want-a-career-not-just-a-job-summit-told

Byrne, D. (1971). *Attraction paradigm.* New York, NY: Academic Press.

Chan, H., Wan, L. C., & Sin, L. Y. (2009). The contrasting effects of culture on consumer tolerance: Interpersonal face and impersonal fate. *Journal of Consumer Research, 36*(2), 292–304. doi:10.1086/597329

Cordesman, A. H. (2003). *Saudi Arabia enters the twenty-first century: The political, foreign policy, economic, and energy dimensions.* Westport, CT: Praeger.

Cunningham, R., & Sarayrah, Y. (1993). *Wasta: The hidden force in Middle Eastern society.* Westport, CT: Praeger.

Doha News (2011, December 4). FT: Tackle Qatarization by adding more women to the payroll. *Doha News.* Retrieved from http://dohanews.co/

Doha News (2013, May 13). Survey: Gulf-wide nationalization efforts face similar stumbling blocks. *Doha News.* Retrieved from http://dohanews.co/

DWE (Dubai Women Establishment) (2009). *Arab women: Leadership outlook 2009-2011.* Retrieved from www.pwc.com/en_GX/gx/women-at-pwc/ assets/Arab-Women-Leadership-Outlook.pdf

Earley, C., & Mosakowski, E. (2000). Creating hybrid team cultures: An empirical test of transnational team functioning. *Academy of Management Journal, 43*(1), 26–49. doi:10.2307/1556384

Fatany, S. (2014, December 5). Saudization shouldn't compromise international standards. *Saudi News.* Retrieved from www.saudigazette.com.sa/index. cfm?method=home.regcon&contentid=201412062265655

Feghali, E. (1997). Arab cultural communication patterns. *International Journal of Intercultural Relations, 21*(3), 345–378. doi:10.1016/S0147-1767(97) 00005-9

Forstenlechner, I., & Rutledge, E. J. (2011). The GCC's "demographic imbalance": Perceptions, realities, and policy options. *Middle East Policy, 18*(4), 25–43. doi:10.1111/j.1475-4967.2011.00508.x

Goby, V. P. (2015). Financialization and outsourcing in a different guise: The ethical chaos of workforce localization in the United Arab Emirates. *Journal of Business Ethics, 131*(2), 415–421. doi:10.1007/s10551-014-2285-6

Goby, V. P., & Nickerson, C. (2015a). The impact of culture on the construal of organizational crisis: Perceptions of crisis in Dubai. *Corporate Communications: An International Journal, 20*(3), 310–325. doi:10.1108/CCIJ-06-2014-0036

Goby, V. P., & Nickerson, C. (2015b). Multicultural and multilingual: Workplace communication in Dubai. In N. Holden, S. Michailova, & S. Tietze (Eds.), *The Routledge companion to cross-cultural management* (pp. 103–111). London, UK: Routledge.

Goby, V. P., Nickerson, C., & David, E. (2015). Interpersonal communication and diversity climate: Promoting workforce localization in the UAE. *International Journal of Organizational Analysis, 23*(3), 364–377. doi:10.1108/IJOA-09-2014-0796

Goffman, E. (1955). On face-work: An analysis of ritual elements of social interaction. *Psychiatry: Journal for the Study of Interpersonal Processes, 18*(3), 213–231.

Gurnett, K. (2012, August 3). Why keeping track of your employees is so last century [Web blog post]. Retrieved from www.brazen.com/blog/archive/on-the-job/why-keeping-track-of-your-employees-every-move-is-so-last-century/

Haase, F. A. (2013). Functions of the concept "Arab World": Case studies of English-speaking business communication patterns. *Entelequia: Revista interdisciplinar*, (16), 157–176. Retrieved from www.eumed.net/entelequia/pdf/2013/e16a09.pdf

Haase, F. A. (2014, May 2). Contrastive studies in communication styles of Gulf Arab business culture and Western business communication cultures. Retrieved from http://ssrn.com/abstract=1937092

Hall, E. (1976). *Beyond culture.* New York, NY: Anchor Books.

Hall, E. T. (1966). *The hidden dimension.* New York, NY: Anchor Books.

Halligan, P. (2006). Caring for patients of Islamic denomination: Critical care nurses' experiences in Saudi Arabia. *Journal of Clinical Nursing, 15*(12), 1565–1573. doi:10.1111/j.1365-2702.2005.01525.x

Haque, F. (2014, February 18). 100,000 expats to lose jobs in Omanisation. *Times of Oman.* Retrieved from www.timesofoman.com/News/29950/Article-100-000-expats-to-lose-jobs-in-Omanisation

Harry, W. (2007). Employment creation and localization: The crucial human resource issues for the GCC. *International Journal of Human Resource Management, 18*(1), 132–146. doi:10.1080/09585190601068508

Hatim, B. (1990). A model of argumentation from Arabic rhetoric: Insights for a theory of text types. *British Journal of Middle Eastern Studies, 17*(1), 47–54. doi:10.1080/13530199008705505

Hawley, D. (2000). *The Trucial states.* Norwich, England: Michael Russell Publishing.

Herb, M. (2009). A nation of bureaucrats: Political participation and economic diversification in Kuwait and the United Arab Emirates. *International Journal of Middle East Studies, 41*(3), 375–395.

Hertog, S. (2012). A comparative assessment of labor market nationalization policies in the GCC. In S. Hertog (Ed.) National employment, migration and education in the GCC. *The Gulf Region: Economic development and diversification,* 4. Berlin, Germany: Gerlach Press. ISBN 9783940924001.

Hertog, S. (2013). *The private sector and reform in the Gulf Cooperation Council.* Retrieved from www.lse.ac.uk/middleEastCentre/kuwait/documents/The-private-sector-and-reform-in-the-GCC.pdf

Hertog, S. (2014). State and private sector in the GCC after the Arab uprisings. *Journal of Arabian Studies, 3*(2), 174–195. doi:10.1080/21534764.2013.86 3678

Hofstede, G. (1980). *Culture's consequences: International differences in work-related values.* Beverly Hills, CA: Sage Publications.

Hofstede, G. (2011). Dimensionalizing cultures: The Hofstede model in context. *Online Readings in Psychology and Culture, 2*(1). doi:10.9707/2307-0919.1014

Holland, T. (2013). *In the shadow of the sword.* London, UK: Abacus.

House, R. J., Hanges, P. J., Javidan, M., Dorfman, P. W., & Gupta, V. (2004). *Leadership, culture, and organizations: The GLOBE study of 62 societies.* Thousand Oaks, CA: Sage Publications.

Jamali, D., Sidani, Y., & Safieddine, A. (2005). Constraints facing working women in Lebanon: An insider view. *Women in Management Review, 20*(8), 581–594. doi:10.1108/09649420510635213

Johnstone-Koch, B. (1983). Presentation as proof: The language of Arabic rhetoric. *Anthropological Linguistics, 25,* 47–60.

Johnstone-Koch, B. (1987). Parataxis in Arabic: Modification as a model for persuasion. *Studies in Language, 11,* 85–98.

Johnstone-Koch, B. (1990). "Orality" and discourse structure in modern standard Arabic. In M. Eid (Ed.), *New perspectives on Arabic linguistics, Vol. 1* (pp. 215–233). Philadelphia, PA: John Benjamins.

Jones, S. (2007). Training and cultural context in the Arab Emirates: Fighting a losing battle? *Employee Relations, 30*(1), 48–62. doi:10.1108/01425450 810835419

Kabasakal, H., & Bodur, M. (2002). Arabic cluster: A bridge between East and West. *Journal of World Business, 37*(1), 40–54. doi:10.1016/S1090-9516(01)00073-6

Kaplan, R. B. (2011). Cultural thought patterns. In T. Silva & P. K. Matsuda (Eds.), *Landmark essays on ESL writing, Vol. 17* (pp. 11–25). New York, NY & London: Routledge.

Kassem, M., & Habib, G. (1989). *Strategic management of services in the Arab Gulf States: Company and industry cases.* New York, NY: De Gruyter.

Knight, J. G., Mitchell, B. S., & Gao, H. (2009). Riding out the Muhammad cartoons crisis: Contrasting strategies and outcomes. *Long Range Planning, 42*(1), 6–22. doi:10.1016/j.lrp.2008.11.002

Locker, K. O., & Kaczmarek, S. K. (2013). *Business communication: Building critical skills.* London, UK: McGraw Hill.

Looney, R. E. (1992). Man-power options in a small labour-importing state: The influence of ethnic composition on Kuwait's development. *International Migration, 30*(2), 175–200. doi:10.1111/j.1468-2435.1992.tb00692.x

Loosemore, M., & Al Muslmani, H. S. (1999). Construction project management in the Persian Gulf: Inter-cultural communication. *International Journal of Project Management, 17*(2), 95–100. doi:10.1016/S0263-7863(98)00030-1

Louhiala-Salminen, L., Charles, M., & Kankaanranta, A. (2005). English as a lingua franca in Nordic corporate mergers: Two case companies. *English for Specific Purposes, 24*(4), 401–421. doi:10.1016/j.esp.2005.02.003

Maddy-Weitzman, B. A. (Ed.) (1997). *Middle East contemporary survey, Vol. XIX, 1995.* Boulder, CO: Westview Press.

Marois, T. (2012). *States, banks, and crisis: Emerging finance capitalism in Mexico and Turkey.* Cheltenham, UK: Edward Elgar.

McGinley, S. (2012, January 15). Qatar alcohol ban could be tip of the iceberg for GCC [Web blog post]. Retrieved from www.arabianbusiness.com/qatar-alcohol-ban-could-be-tip-of-iceberg-for-gcc-440454.html

Mehlum, H., & Ostensad, G. (2011). *Migration into resource-rich Gulf economies.* Retrieved from www.isid.ac.in/~pu/conference/dec_11_conf/Papers/GryOstenstad.pdf

Merchant, N. (2011). Google, don't choose micromanagement [Web blog post]. Retrieved from https://hbr.org/2011/04/google-dont-choose-micromanage

Millington, B. (2009, January 29). Bahrainisation driving black market visas: Contractor. *ConstructionWeekOnline.* Retrieved from www.constructionweek online.com/article-4273-bahrainisation-driving-black-market-visas-contractor/

Mostafa, M. M. (2004). Attitudes towards women managers in the United Arab Emirates: The effects of patriarchy, age, and sex differences. *Journal of Managerial Psychology, 20*(5/6), 522–540. doi:10.1108/02683940510615451

Munck, B. (2001, November). Changing a culture of face time. *Harvard Business Review*. Retrieved from https://hbr.org/2001/11/changing-a-culture-of-face-time

Munif, A. (2002, April 8). Gulf population growth rate highest in world. *Gulf News*. http://gulfnews.com/news/uae/general/gulf-population-growth-rate-highest-in-world-1.384001

Mustafa, H. (2013, September 5). Saudization program not helping Saudi Arabia's economic "competitiveness." *Al Arabiya News*. Retrieved from http://english.alarabiya.net/en/business/economy/2013/09/05/Saudization-program-not-helping-Saudi-Arabia-s-economic-competitiveness-.html

Nagy Eltony, M. (2007). The economic development experience of Kuwait: Some useful lessons. *Journal of Economic and Administrative Sciences*, *23*(1), 77–102. doi:10.1108/10264116200700003

Natividad, I. (2010). *Corporate women directors international 2010 report: Accelerating board diversity globally*. Retrieved from www.europarl.europa.eu/document/activities/cont/201011/20101124ATT00354/20101124ATT00354EN.pdf

Nickerson, C., & Goby, V. P. (2016). Exploring female leadership communication in the United Arab Emirates: Issues of culture and gender. In C. Ilie & S. Schuur (Eds.), *Leadership stereotypes: Discourse and power management*. London, UK: Springer.

Planken, B. (2005). Managing rapport in lingua franca sales negotiations: A comparison of professional and aspiring negotiators. *English for Specific Purposes*, *24*(4), 381–400. doi:10.1108/02683940510615451

Poyatos, F. (1983). *New perspectives in nonverbal communication: Studies in cultural anthropology, social psychology, linguistics, literature, and semiotics* (Vol. 5). Oxford, UK: Pergamon.

Randall, M., & Samimi, M. A. (2010). The status of English in Dubai. *English Today*, *26*(1), 43–50. doi:10.1017/S0266078409990617

Rapanta, C., & Badran, D. (2015). Same but different: Perceptions of interpersonal arguing in two Arabic populations (UAE and Lebanon). *Journal of Media Critiques*, *1*(2), 119–131. doi:10.17349/jmc115109

Rapanta, C., & Hample, D. (2015). Orientations to interpersonal arguing in the United Arab Emirates, with comparisons to the United States, China, and India. *Journal of Intercultural Communication Research*, *44*(4), 263–287. doi: 10.1080/17475759.2015.1081392

Rejimon, K. (2014, November 10). Upcoming labour law to boost jobs in Oman. *Times of Oman*. Retrieved from www.timesofoman.com/News/42556/Article-Upcoming-labour-law-to-boost-jobs-in-Oman

Rogerson-Revell, P. (2010). Can you spell that for us non-native speakers?: Accommodation strategies in international business meetings. *Journal of Business Communication*, *47*(4), 432–454. doi:10.1177/0021943610377304

Salem, O. (2010, December 11). Firms face big fines for "ghost Emiratization." *The National.* Retrieved from www.thenational.ae/news/uae-news/firms-face-big-fines-for-ghost-emiratisation

Salem, O., & Dajani, H. (2013, November 19). FNC would like Emiratisation to become law. *The National.* Retrieved from www.thenational.ae/uae/government/fnc-would-like-emiratisation-to-become-law

Salzman, P. C. (2008). *Culture and conflict in the Middle East.* Amherst, NY: Humanity Books.

Schwab, K. (2015). *Global Competitiveness Report.* Geneva: World Economic Forum. Retrieved from www3.weforum.org/docs/WEF_GlobalCompetitivenessReport_2014-15.pdf

Scott-Jackson, W. (2010). *The Gulf Arab management style as a source of strategic advantage: Building global strategic capabilities on the foundations of local culture.* Retrieved from www.cahrr.org/human-resources-research/material/Scott-JacksonGulfArabMgmtStyles.pdf

Simpson, R. (1998). Presenteeism, power and organizational change: Long hours as a career barrier and the impact on the working lives of women managers. *British Journal of Management, 9*(1), 37–50. doi:10.1111/1467-8551.9.s1.5

Smith, P. B., Achoui, M., & Harb, C. (2007). Unity and diversity in Arab management styles. *International Journal of Cross Cultural Management, 7*(3), 275–290. doi:10.1177/1470595807083374

Spencer-Oatey, H. (2000). Rapport management: A framework for analysis. In H. Spencer-Oatey, (Ed.), *Culturally speaking: Managing rapport through talk across cultures* (pp. 11–46). London, UK: Continuum.

Swailes, S., Al Said, L. G., & Al Fahdi, S. (2012). Localisation policy in Oman: A psychological contracting interpretation. *International Journal of Public Sector Management, 25*(5), 357–372. doi:10.1108/09513551211252387

Tamkeen. 2006. www.lf.bh/en/

Tlaiss, H. A. (2013). Women managers in the United Arab Emirates: Successful careers or what? *Equality, Diversity and Inclusion: An International Journal, 32*(8), 756–776. doi:10.1108/EDI-12-2012-0109

Trenwith, C. (2013, November 12). Emiratisation failing to cut UAE jobless rate – Al Mulla. *Arabian Business.* Retrieved from www.arabianbusiness.com/emiratisation-failing-cut-uaejobless-rate-al-mulla-526191.html

Trompenaars, F. (1994). *Riding the waves of culture: Understanding the diversity in global business.* New York, NY: Irwin Publishing.

Tsui, A. S., & O'Reilly, C. A. (1989). Beyond simple demographic effects: The importance of relational demography in superior-subordinate dyads. *Academy of Management Journal, 32*(2), 402–423. doi:10.2307/256368

Turner, L. H., & West, R. L. (2010). *Introducing communication theory: Analysis and application* (4th ed.). New York, NY: McGraw-Hill.

Walker, L. (2014, 25 August). New panel established to push private sector to employ more Qataris. *Doha News*. Retrieved from http://dohanews.co/panel-push-private-sector-employ-qatari-nationals/

WEF, (2014). *The global gender gap report 2014*. Geneva: World Economic Forum. Retrieved from www3.weforum.org/docs/GGGR14/GGGR_CompleteReport_2014.pdf

Weiss, C. E. (1998). Negotiating with foreign business persons: An introduction for Americans with propositions on six cultures. In S. Niemeier, C. P. Campbell, & R. Dirven (Eds.), *The cultural context in business communication* (pp. 51–118). Philadelphia: Benjamin.

Women in the United Arab Emirates: A portrait of progress. (2009). Retrieved from http://lib.ohchr.org/HRBodies/UPR/Documents/Session3/AE/UPR_UAE_ANNEX3_E.pdf

Wu, R. T-Y., Fey, Y-H., Tsai, M-H., & Wu, F. T. (2006). A Study of the relationship between manager's leadership style and organizational commitment in Taiwan's international tourist hotels. *Asian Journal of Management and Humanity Sciences, 1*(3), 434–452.

Yaseen, Z. (2010). Leadership styles of men and women in the Arab world. *Education, Business and Society: Contemporary Middle Eastern Issues, 3*(1), 63–70. doi:10.1108/17537981011022823

Zaharna, R. S. (1995). Bridging cultural differences: American public relations practices & Arab communication patterns. *Public Relations Review, 21*(3), 241–255. doi:10.1016/0363-8111(95)90024-1

Zane, N., & Yeh, M. (2002). The use of culturally-based variables in assessment: Studies on loss of face. In K. Kurasaki, S. Okazaki, & S. Sue (Eds.), *Asian American mental health: Assessment theories and methods* (pp. 123–140). Dordrecht, Netherland: Kluwer Academic.

Zeffane, R. (1995). Organizational commitment and perceived management styles: The public-private sector contrast. *Management Research News, 18*(6/7), 9–20. www.emeraldinsight.com/journals.htm?articleid=1647856

Index

OTHER TITLES IN OUR CORPORATE COMMUNICATION COLLECTION

Debbie DuFrene, Stephen F. Austin State University, Editor

- *The Language of Success: The Confidence and Ability to Say What You Mean and Mean What You Say in Business and Life* by Kim Wilkerson and Alan Weiss
- *Writing for Public Relations: A Practical Guide for Professionals* by Janet Mizrahi
- *SPeak Performance: Using the Power of Metaphors to Communicate Vision, Motivate People, and Lead Your Organization to Success* by Jim Walz
- *Today's Business Communication: A How-To Guide for the Modern Professional* by Jason L. Snyder and Robert Forbus
- *Leadership Talk: A Discourse Approach to Leader Emergence* by Robyn Walker and Jolanta Aritz
- *Communication Beyond Boundaries* by Payal Mehra
- *Managerial Communication* by Reginald L. Bell and Jeanette S. Martin
- *Writing for the Workplace: Business Communication for Professionals* by Janet Mizrahi
- *Get Along, Get It Done, Get Ahead: Interpersonal Communication in the Diverse Workplace* by Geraldine E. Hynes
- *Managing Virtual Teams, Second Edition* by Debbie D. DuFrene and Carol M. Lehman

Announcing the Business Expert Press Digital Library

Concise e-books business students need for classroom and research

This book can also be purchased in an e-book collection by your library as

- a one-time purchase,
- that is owned forever,
- allows for simultaneous readers,
- has no restrictions on printing, and
- can be downloaded as PDFs from within the library community.

Our digital library collections are a great solution to beat the rising cost of textbooks. E-books can be loaded into their course management systems or onto students' e-book readers.
The **Business Expert Press** digital libraries are very affordable, with no obligation to buy in future years. For more information, please visit **www.businessexpertpress.com/librarians**. To set up a trial in the United States, please email **sales@businessexpertpress.com**.

www.ingramcontent.com/pod-product-compliance
Lightning Source LLC
Chambersburg PA
CBHW071213200326
41519CB00018B/5508